SANTA DOLLS

A celebration of Father Christmas doll art,
both antique and contemporary

by Ann Bahar

Published by Hobby House Press, Inc.
Cumberland, Maryland 21502

For Sonya, Robert, Daniel
and especially
for Leon

Cover Description: "Santa in The Moon" by
Rosemary Volpi. See page 132 for further infor-
mation.

Additional copies of this book may be purchased at $29.95
from
HOBBY HOUSE PRESS
900 Frederick Street
Cumberland, Maryland 21502
or from your favorite bookstore or dealer.
Please add $5.50 per copy for postage.

©1992 Ann Bahar

Printed in the United States of America

ISBN: 0-87588-397-4

Table of Contents

Introduction

Of the many Christmas books published in recent years, almost all focus exclusively on the past, with its wealth of antique toys, dolls, fragile glass ornaments, old holiday greeting cards, paper scraps and dog-eared scrapbooks — survivors of damp, dust, mice and two World Wars that provide nostalgic reminders for us moderns of what Christmas was like in "the good old days." That little has been written about Christmas art as an ongoing tradition is regrettable, since there are dozens of American doll artists at work today for whom the holiday provides a very special kind of inspiration. They are the Santa doll artists of the 1980s and 1990s, talented craftspersons for whom Father Christmas lore and antique artifacts provide a unique springboard for their own highly-individual creative drive.

Here is a book of old and new Father Christmas dolls crafted in paper, wood, papier-mâché, metal, cloth, Fimo® — almost every conceivable medium and from every imaginable perspective. It is an ingathering of images from today and yesterday, an effort to provide everyone for whom the magic of Christmas conjures up the face of Santa Claus with an overview of the incredible variety of dolls and display figures that remarkable character has inspired over the years. It is a first attempt to provide a generous sampler in text and pictures of Santa dolls crafted in the past and today, a one-stop introduction to the doll artists' Christmas Man.

We hope everyone who loves the holiday season, along with collectors of Christmas dolls and toys, will agree with the artist who told the author: "When I first started to craft Father Christmas dolls, I looked for this book. It wasn't out there, and I'm very glad it will be now!"

In Appreciation...

Without advice, assistance and photographs contributed by hundreds of artists, collectors, dealers, scholars, friends and family members, this book could not have been written.

Thanks are due to David Franks and Kathleen Banks in England, and to Dorothy Hesner of Cicero, Illinois, who shared paper treasures from Mamelok Press archives and their personal collections. Also to John Grafton of Dover Publications, Inc; to Albert Louer, Ann Watkins and Cathy Grosfils of The Colonial Williamsburg Foundation; to Claudia Brigg of Christie's Colour Library in London; to Margaret Munday Whitaker and The Lilliput Museum of Antique Dolls and Toys (Isle of Wight, United Kingdom); to Sheila Bradley of Swanson's Auctions in Mountain Center, California; to Butterfield and Butterfield in San Francisco; and to Marguerite Fawdry at Pollock's Toy Museum on Scala Street in London, England.

Ann Parker advised us of the singular lack of Santa doll artists in today's United Kingdom, and Ingeborg Riesser sent similar news regarding the state of the art in France, which made possible the claim that Father Christmas doll making is a peculiarly American preoccupation.

We are grateful to Dr. and Mrs. James Ellis and a chance meeting in Swarthmore. Thanks also go to Barbara S. Koelle, Betty Rossi, Barbara Spears and Paige Thornton, to Frank Hanley, Jefferey Guéno and to our good friend Tom Roberts; also to Paul Pilgrim, Inge Riesser, Lois Clarkson, Susan Brown Nicholson, Terry Michaud, Patricia N. Schoonmaker, Rosemary Volpp and Donna Harrison. Help was offered by David Bausch of Allentown, Pennsylvania, by Ron Benson, Ellen Krucker Blauer, Beverly Port, Eleanor LaVove of Angels Attic Museum in Santa Monica, California, and Nat Roth of the Furman Roth Advertising Agency in New York City. We are grateful to Philip F. Mooney, Archivist for the Coca-Cola® Company in Atlanta, Georgia; to Sarah Salisbury for advice about Santa dolls in dollhouse scale; to Margaret Whitton, who encouraged this project and shared treasures from her library and personal collection.

A big "thank you"' to Krystyna Poray Goddu in New York, who first recognized that Santa dolls, old and new, were waiting to be published and that collectors and lovers of Christmas everywhere might welcome the event.

We owe an incalculable debt to Carolyn Cook, Donna Felger and Margot Skelley at Hobby House Press, Inc.; also to photographer and longtime friend Peter Groesbeck of Philadelphia, Pennsylvania, whose talent, patience and welcome sense of humor have done so much to bring the Santa doll story to life. Thanks too, to Betty Barbara Smart of the Swarthmore Public Library in Swarthmore, Pennsylvania, for invaluable assistance during months of research, and to the dozens and dozens of gifted artists who share their work and their histories through these pages.

Finally, heartfelt thanks to my beloved family for encouragement and advice during the hectic months when Santa Claus boarded at our house. Yes, Leon, the experience did indeed have its difficult moments. But it sure was fun!

The Making of a Tradition: Santa Claus, His Story

Today's Father Christmas doll artist faces a nearly overwhelming abundance of history, legend and artifacts from which to draw inspiration. There are old Father Christmas dolls and toys and thousands of quaint old advertisements and antique holiday postcards that picture every imaginable permutation of the familiar figure. There are marvelous old German, French and American chocolate and ice cream molds, key sources for outstanding 20th century chalkware and papier-mâché Santa designers. Surviving 19th-century glass tree ornaments and new ornaments cast from antique molds, then finished according to traditional methods, contribute to our own century's awareness of the bewildering multiplicity of faces and attitudes that characterized Father Christmas in days of yore!

Behind the Santa art of today and yesterday lives the old, old story of good Saint Nicholas, the 4th century Bishop of Myra, who tossed bags of gold through open windows (some say down chimneys!), saved sailors from shipwreck, protected children, merchants, thieves and the poor. The Saint's complex history grew even more complex when his tomb was ransacked by 11th-century zealots who carried the holy bones to southern Italy where they became the focus of a holy shrine at Bari. Years later, the Norman French brought a single bone from Bari to Lorraine, and Saint Nicholas worship became a magnet for devout pilgrims within Europe.

Saint Nicholas Day (December 6th), Christmas and a tangle of pre-Christian winter festival myths — the divine nature of evergreens, year-end sacrifice to insure the new year's harvest, the mystique of mistletoe, straw dolls, straw bundles, elves, gnomes and other mischief makers — commingle as we follow the extraordinary story down the centuries and watch it change, evolve and ultimately fuse with innumerable local cultures. The tale owes a debt to the Lapps and Finns who first hitched reindeer to the magic sleigh, to Thor and Freya (gods of Norse mythology) for the pigs and goats with which Father Christmas is frequently pictured, to Swedish *nisse* (household elves) for Santa's elfin stature and to the Coca-Cola® Company, whose enormously successful 1930s-1950s Christmas ads featuring Haddon Sundblom's Santa Clauses completed Saint Nick's metamorphosis into the larger-than-life Christmas friend we moderns take for granted.

When Christianity arrived in Northern Europe in the 6th century, the clergy found it expedient to combine existing pagan with new Christian festivals, and as the *Bible* nowhere states the precise date of Christ's birth, the event was celebrated in conjunction with local winter festivals of sacrifice, rebirth and renewal that have typified agricultural societies since time immemorial.

A millennium later, the Protestant Reformation deplored the wild behavior that had become acceptable Christmas holiday-making. As a consequence, the religious and secular elements of Christmas split. On the secular side, curious hybrid figures evolved, — gift givers with strange, occasionally fearsome faces, figures symbolic of Time, of jollity, of Baccanalian excess, of love. In Italy, there was Befana, an aged peasant woman who, according to legend, refused to follow the Magi in their journey to Bethlehem and was condemned to wander the earth forever in a fruitless search for the Christ Child. Befana's counterpart in pre-revolutionary Russia was Babouschka, another old woman who seeks the Holy Infant each December, leaving presents for the boys and girls whose homes she enters. Babouschka's tenuous link to Christian orthodoxy worried Russia's communist leaders who substituted the less-controversial winter gift giver of Russian folklore, Father Frost. In today's U.S.S.R., where cultural and political upheaval seems a daily occurrence and the Church is once again sanctioned, one wonders what shape the Christmas figure will ultimately take.

The Protestant Reformation in Germany gave the world Pelsnickle (literally "Nicholas in Furs") as well as the savage Knecht Ruprecht; in France, Père Noël took his first bow. In Holland, Saint Nicholas retained his ancient Bishop's robes and miter but gained a companion named Black Peter, a satanic character whose Spanish Renaissance costume echoes the days when Hapsburgs ruled the Low Countries.

With the passage of years, fascinating new figures emerged to embellish the evolving tradition. There was the mystical Christkindl, a gift-giver child dressed in white, surrounded by heavenly light and usually depicted walking barefoot in a wintry wasteland. In the 19th century, the letters of the Christkind's name regrouped to give the world Kris Kringle. The Dutch brought a secularized Saint Nicholas and his Saint's Day to the New World, and when the Duke of York claimed New Amsterdam for the English King in 1664, Dutch Sinter Claes began his most recent transformation into the jolly Santa of today.

The 19th century, with its incredibly rapid advances in industrialization, literacy, communication and travel comfort, literally pulled hundreds of local Father Christmas traditions out of the colorful geographic pockets in which they had grown up and made them accessible to everyone, everywhere, as part of the sea of printed paper that flooded the age. Today's Santa artists find inspiration in the explosion of storybooks, illustrations, cartoons and paper ephemera that characterized the last century. Much of this material has survived to thrill us moderns as it thrilled our ancestors, whose "brave new world" was a gorgeous web of printed words and brilliant color work.

In that tangled jungle of type and ink, Santa debuted in 1809, with American author Washington Irving's publication of *Knickerbocker's History of New York*. Irving's witty pen and gentle humor metamorphosed the Saint into a delightful Dutch burgher who wears wide pantaloons and smokes a miracle-working long-stemmed white clay pipe. In 1822, Clement Clark Moore, again a New Yorker, composed "A Visit from Saint Nicholas" as a Christmas treat for his children. The piece was published the following year in the Troy, New York *Sentinel* and was issued in book form for the first time in 1848. Moore's description of Santa Claus "dressed all in fur from his head to his foot" was interpreted freely by various illustrators, beginning with John Gadsby Chapman in 1840. But it was left for Thomas Nast to combine the jolly, pipe-smoking Dutchman and the Father Christmas of his Bavarian childhood with Moore's word pictures to create the modern Santa Claus.

No account of the growing importance of the Christmas season, and with it of the figure that symbolizes it, is complete without mention of Dickens' Christmas writings, in *Pickwick* and in his familiar and less-familiar Christmas stories. The best-known of these is, of course, *A Christmas Carol* (1843) where the Ghost of Christmas Past is reminiscent of the German Christkindl, the Ghost of Christmas

Present, immortalized by John Leech's magnificent illustrations, echoes the Spirit-of-the-Season Christmas Man who runs riot through 19th-century holiday publications; and the Ghost of Christmas Future dots the "i's" and crosses the "t's" of what is, after all, one of literature's finest morality plays.

Since Dickens' day, Father Christmas has played bit parts and lead roles in innumerable literary works. Thus, Santa stars in Florence Upton's 1907 classic, *The Golliwog's Christmas* and in L. Frank Baum's *Life and Adventures of Santa Claus* published in 1902. In Howard R. Garis's *Uncle Wiggily's Holidays* (1919), the Old Rabbit Gentleman takes over Santa's job, as does Babar the elephant in Jean de Brunhoff's 1930s masterpiece *Babar and Father Christmas*. In addition to its famous Santa covers, December numbers of the venerable *Saint Nicholas* magazine published a stream of stories awash in Victorian sentiment. They included "How Santa Claus Found The Poor-House" by Sophie Swett, "Leonard's English Christmas" by Alice Hegan Rice and "My Grandmother's Grandmother's Christmas Candle" by Hezekiah Butterworth, as well as brilliantly crafted charmers like William Dean Howells' comic satirical "Christmas Every Day."

Among Santa's hundreds of appearances in the fiction of past decades, one of the finest, surely, is the exquisite role he plays in C.S. Lewis's 1950 blend of fantasy, religion and whimsy, *The Lion, The Witch and The Wardrobe*, the first volume in *The Chronicles of Narnia*. At a critical moment in the story, when luck seems about to run out altogether and the triumph of evil seems inescapable, sleigh bells jingle and Father Christmas arrives to unlock the magic that leads to the story's glorious conclusion. Of course, Father Christmas's sledge is pulled by reindeer. But, the author informs us, "they were far bigger than the Witch's reindeer, and they were not white but brown. And on the sledge sat a person whom everyone knew the minute they set eyes on him. He was a huge man in a bright red robe (bright as holly-berries) with a hood that had fur inside it and a great white beard that fell like a foamy waterfall over his chest. Everyone knew him because, though you see people of his sort only in Narnia, you see pictures of them and hear them talked about even in our world..." Who, among today's Santa doll artists, can resist the temptation to "hit the clay" after reading this gorgeous passage!

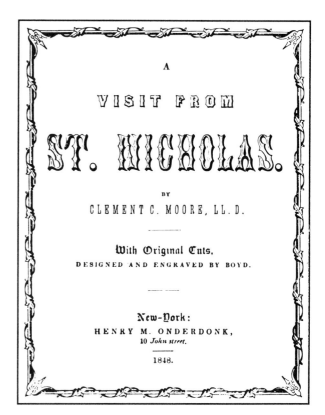

Clement Clark Moore (1779-1863), whose poem, *A Visit from St. Nicholas*, was the genesis of the modern Santa Claus. From *The Night Before Christmas* (reprinted by Dover Publications, Inc., 1971). *Reproduced with the permission of the publisher.*

Facsimile of the title page of the first (1848) book-format rendering of Clement Moore's immortal poem. From *The Night Before Christmas* (reprinted by Dover Publications, Inc., 1971). *Reproduced with the permission of the publisher.*

The first (1848) book format edition of *A Visit from St. Nicholas* was illustrated by a New York wood engraver named T.C. Boyd. Modern readers, accustomed to Nast's Santa Claus and his modern cousins, are often startled by the work of earlier artists. From *The Night Before Christmas* (reprinted by Dover Publications, Inc., 1971). *Reproduced with the permission of the publisher.*

One of Santa's first bows in American children's literature, *Kriss Kringle's Christmas Tree*, was published in Philadelphia in 1845. *Library of Congress photograph. Reproduced with permission.*

The Spirit of Christmas presiding at the holiday feast, a scene from Webb's toy theater production titled "Harlequin's Jack and The Beanstalk." An example of this gorgeous, tinselled-paper confection, which echoed the Drury Lane Christmas pantomime of 1860, is preserved in the famous collection of Pollock's Toy Museum in London. *Photograph courtesy of Pollock's Toy Museum. London, England.*

Large cotton kerchief, block-printed by The Oriental Print Works. The piece measures 17in (43cm) by 23½in (60cm) and derives from Peck's cloth doll design issued by the same firm in the 1880s. *Photograph courtesy of The Abby Aldrich Rockefeller Folk Art Center, Williamsburg, Virginia.*

ABOVE LEFT: The Christmas Fairy represents the ultimate secularization of the Father Christmas scenario. In this old chromos, the Fairy is costumed like a ballerina and spills holiday goodies from a magic stocking. *Photograph by Peter Groesbeck. Courtesy of Mamelok Press Ltd.*

ABOVE: In Victorian England, the robin, subject of innumerable tales of mercy, kindness and Christian love, was a beloved symbol of the holiday. Charming English robins, each with a splash of crimson on its downy front, were among the most popular motifs for seasonal scraps and greeting cards. *Photograph by Peter Groesbeck. Courtesy of Mamelok Press Ltd.*

A variant of the Christkindl was the Christmas angel, here shown with a bevy of Victorian youngsters. Note the interlocking symbols. Like Father Christmas, this German-published holiday angel bears gifts and has an evergreen strapped to its back. *Photograph by Peter Groesbeck. Courtesy of Mamelok Press Ltd.*

ABOVE: The Christkindl, a mysterious and lovely gift bearer who first appeared in Germany during the Reformation. *Photograph by Peter Groesbeck. Courtesy of Mamelok Press Ltd.*

ABOVE RIGHT: A curious appearance of the Christkindl, here the frontispiece of the very first issue of England's famous *Strand* magazine. The spirit child is lightly clad, barefoot in a wood and surrounded by a heavenly glow. Compare this rendering to the Christkindl scrap from Mamelok's archival albums (above). *From* The Victorian Christmas Book *by Antony and Peter Miall (J.M. Dent & Sons Ltd., 1978). Reproduced with permission.*

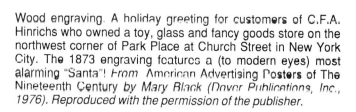

Wood engraving. A holiday greeting for customers of C.F.A. Hinrichs who owned a toy, glass and fancy goods store on the northwest corner of Park Place at Church Street in New York City. The 1873 engraving features a (to modern eyes) most alarming "Santa"! *From* American Advertising Posters of The Nineteenth Century *by Mary Black (Dover Publications, Inc., 1976). Reproduced with the permission of the publisher.*

"For Santa"

Haddon Sundblom's Santas looked down on America from posters distributed across the country from 1930 through the 1950s. How curious that it was the Coca-Cola® Company's inspired idea that completed the metamorphosis of the fourth-century Bishop into the jolly holiday visitor we know today. *Photograph courtesy of The Coca-Cola® Company, Atlanta, Georgia.*

OPPOSITE PAGE: Today in The Netherlands, Saint Nicholas arrives by sea on the last Saturday in November, then rides triumphant through the streets of coastal cities, escorted by smiling (!) Black Peters in Spanish Renaissance dress. Pictured is Saint Nicholas as he enters Amsterdam's main square, amid cheering crowds of delighted youngsters. *Photograph courtesy of the Consulate General of The Netherlands, New York City.*

Haddon Sundblom, the artist behind the famous Coca-Cola® Santas of the 1930s-1950s, at work in his studio. When his delightful model died, Mr. Sundblom became his own model! *Photograph courtesy of The Coca-Cola® Company, Atlanta, Georgia.*

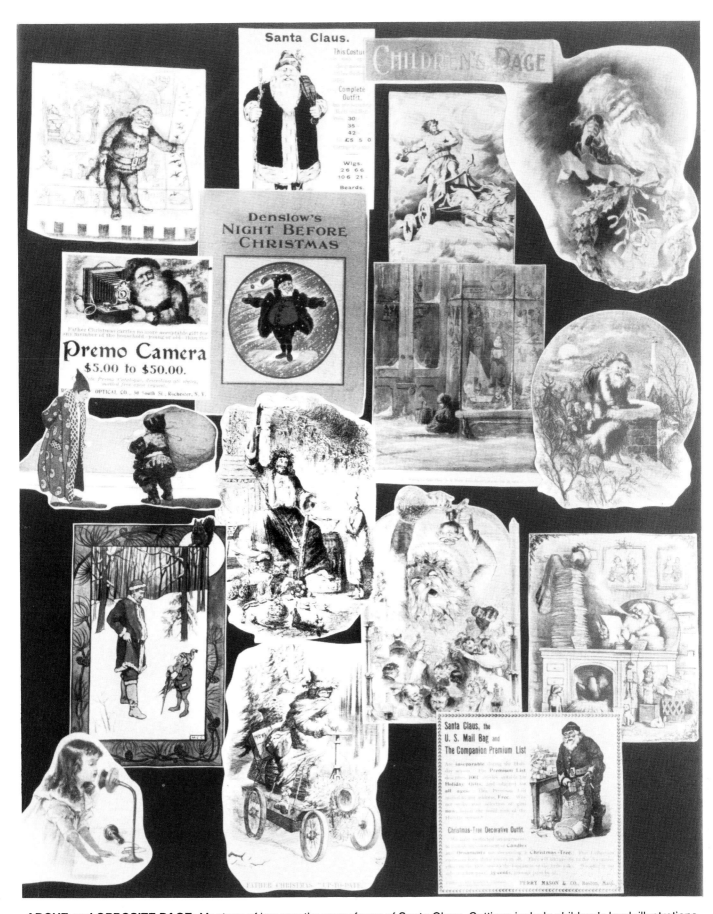

ABOVE and OPPOSITE PAGE: Montage of images: the many faces of Santa Claus. Cuttings include children's book illustrations, work by Nast, Tenniel, John Leech, Denslow, Jessie Willcox Smith and others. Also, cartoons (some savage) from *Punch* and *Harper's Weekly*, advertising art from *The Youth's Companion (1880s-1890s), and more... Photographs by Peter Groesbeck.*

ABOVE LEFT: Illustration from *Santa Claus and His Works* by George P. Webster and published by McLoughlin Brothers in 1869. Thomas Nast's illustrations show a jolly elf dressed in a one-piece fur suit, a startling figure, very different from the more attractively scaled (and clad!) Coca-Cola® Santa of the 1930s. *From* Thomas Nast's Drawings *(Dover Publications, Inc., 1978). Reproduced with permission.*

ABOVE: Clement Moore's *Night Before Christmas*, the famous 1902 edition illustrated by W.W. Denslow, who is better remembered as the original illustrator of L. Frank Baum's classic *The Wizard of Oz. Photograph by Peter Groesbeck. Courtesy of Barbara S. Koelle.*

Middle-aged Neclaus and elf, from L. Frank Baum's 1902 classic, *The Life and Adventures of Santa Claus*, illustrated by Mary Cowles Clark. In this fantasy, Neclaus's kindness toward children each December earns him the mantle of immortality, which is why, according to Baum, Santa looks so old yet acts so young! *Photograph by Peter Groesbeck. Courtesy of Barbara S. Koelle.*

Florence Upton's Dutch Dolls and their cavalier, still wearing the Santa suit that gives him such grief in the story, dance around their tree in the 1907 classic, *The Golliwog's Christmas*. *Photograph by Peter Groesbeck. Courtesy of Margaret Whitton.*

The gnome-like stature of the Nastian Santa Claus is obvious in this illustration from Jessie Willcox Smith's 1912 edition of *Twas The Night Before Christmas*. You'd be as startled as the homeowner in the picture to encounter such a Saint Nick in your living room! *Photograph by Peter Groesbeck. Courtesy of Barbara S. Koelle.*

Uncle Wiggily Longears, the rabbit hero of Howard R. Garis's immortal storybooks, dons a Santa suit and delivers joy of the season to poor animal boys and girls, in *Uncle Wiggily's Holidays* (1919). *Photograph by Peter Groesbeck.*

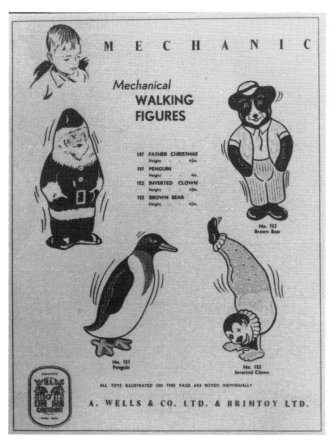

ABOVE: One of ten thousand images of Christmas, this hilarious NUTRI/SYSTEM® poster appeared on the sides of buses across New Jersey in December 1990. *Designed by Furman Roth Advertising Agency, New York City, for Slimline Weight Loss Centers.*

LEFT: A page from A. Wells & Co. & Brimtoy Ltd. circa 1950 trade catalog showing mechanical walking toys, among them a darling tin Santa Claus. *Photograph courtesy of Pollock's Toy Museum, London, England.*

Delicious traditions never die; they just evolve! The Great Chocolate Santa Hunt of December 1990 produced this yummy clutch of molded Clauses made by chocolatiers in Germany, Switzerland, Pennsylvania, Connecticut and Brooklyn, New York. The tallest figure measures 7¾in (20cm). *Photograph by Peter Groesbeck. Courtesy of Author's Kitchen!*

Santa Postcards

Again and again, doll artists we interviewed expressed their debt to long-ago German, French, Belgian, British and American publishers of black-and-white or chromolithographed holiday postcards that brought incredible numbers of 19th and early 20th century Santa images into homes round the globe. Here in the United States there was a voracious market for European-printed greeting cards which became a major United States import before the turn of the century. Thousands of these wonderful old postcard Santas, Père Noëls with French grape baskets strapped to their shoulders, ruddy Father Christmases crowned with holly, dour brown-robed Pelsnickles lugging toy sacks and bundles of switches — have survived the years to inspire artists and thrill collectors in our own time.

The Christmas card, like the postcard and the social letter, owes an enormous debt to a stubborn English visionary, Sir Rowland Hill, who badgered the British Parliament until it adopted his revolutionary new postal system. In 1840, Rowland Hill's brainchild, the Penny Post, was born and changed the world.

Before the Penny Post, mailing fees were paid by the receivers, not the senders of letters. For all but the very rich, the arrival of a holiday mailbag brought with it an unwanted burden of seasonal expense, and among the poorer classes in Britain, more letters were refused than were accepted. It is said that Sir Rowland had the idea for inexpensive *prepaid* letters the day he saw an old cottager's wife refuse a letter from her own son. As of 1840, a letter sent anywhere within Great Britain cost the sender one easily affordable copper penny, and after 1870, when the government first allowed postcard mailings, the minimal cost dropped by half. The number of letters mailed in Britain between 1840 and 1845 increased from 170 to 300 million, and fortunes were made hand-over-fist in the rapidly expanding letter paper and greeting card industries.

The first Christmas card was designed by J.C. Horsley in 1843, as a novel holiday greeting from Sir Henry Cole to his friends and relatives. (Note: London's Victoria and Albert Museum has reissued this historic collector piece as an inexpensive modern postcard.) By the 1860s, Christmas cards, many of which continued to echo features of the fanciful *cartes de visite* and stationery letterhead tradition from which they derived, had become big business. And once legislation approved the postcard as a legitimate form of communication at half price, Victorian publishers flooded a welcoming market with holiday greetings. There were Christmas robins and lace-framed skating scenes, angels, kissing couples beneath mistletoe, snowmen and snowy landscapes, children at prayer and at play, coaches, inn yards, red-cheeked Pickwicks, dancing plum puddings and weeping piglets bearing boars' heads on enormous salvers. Ingenious transformation cards concealed full-color surprises made visible when the cards were held to the light. Die-cut shaped cards were made in the form of people, houses, floral bouquets, diptychs and triptychs. Cards, called in their day "transparencies," depicted churches and cozy rural cottages whose windows glowed with tinted cellophane warmth when held against candle or gas light.

And for the joy of the contemporary buying public and (unbeknownst to their designers) the inspiration of dozens of 20th-century doll artists, there were thousands upon thousands of Santa Claus greeting cards. Many, published in continental Europe or by continental publishers for the English-speaking market, depicted the French Père Noël or the German Pelsnickle, lean and elderly in long robes and peaked hood, with drooping gray whiskers and melancholic mien. Others featured a noisy, buccolic Spirit of the Feast, a Dickensian, often a Bacchic, Christmas Man with full red cheeks, open mouth and a port-wine-and-pudding manner that would make old Saint Nicholas blush!

Victorian greeting card Santas knock at doors and stuff stockings hung from mantels and nursery bedposts. They roll downhill on wooden sleds and inside giant snowballs, float away in hot-air balloons, pilot turn-of-the-century biplanes and perch quaintly on crescent moons hung high in the night sky. They drive sleighs pulled by robins, horses, donkeys, reindeer, pigs and goats. They are expert riders of penny farthing bicycles and fearless drivers of early touring cars and railway engines. The Victorian imagination, with its innate love of detail, incongruity, ingenuity and fantasy, delighted in developing a world of Father Christmas imagery that provided untold tons of postal joy in its day and has provided collectors with an inexhaustible source of pleasure ever since. Queen Victoria commanded a relative to fill scrapbooks with holiday greeting cards for her delectation. The late Queen Mary (1867-1953) continued the royal tradition, and her collection provides a double record of an evolving industry and Royal Yuletide celebration.

Today, Christmas card collecting is a popular specialization among postcard enthusiasts, but few moderns can hope to match the collection amassed by Victorian Londoner Jonathan King, "the Nestor of all Christmas card collectors who, in addition to trying to buy samples of every card published in his time, even managed to buy up some of the manufacturing firms in the latter half of the 19th century, aimed at possessing a copy of every single design, and gathered a collection of immense proportions, turning his house at Islington into a "museum" of Christmas cards, but even he could not see his dream realized. In the 1890s his collections, weighing...between six and seven tons, included about 163,000 varieties of Christmas cards published between 1862 and 1895, but mainly after 1880.[1] Among these tons of holiday greetings were thousands depicting Father Christmas, designs that today are a major idea source for marvelous Santa dolls and display figures.

The Victorians bequeathed numerous charming memoirs and "recollections" to their 20th-century descendants, and many of these mention the joy with which Father Christmas's face and figure, framed in a rainbow of sentimental chromolithographed gingerbread, was welcomed each December. The child Alison Uttley particularly recalled the importance of one Santa Claus transformation card she received in the 1880s, then lost, and found again years later tucked between pages in her mother's treasured Christmas album. The card showed "two children asleep in a bed....At the foot of the bed hang the empty stockings. We hold this card to the lamplight, and Santa Claus appears with his bag packed with toys. He is leaning over to fill those stockings with a toy horse, a doll, a book and a boat. This piece of evidence was of great significance to me," Mrs. Uttley wrote. "It proved beyond a doubt the existence of Father Christmas. When others jeered and said there was no Santa Claus, I kept silent. I knew he lived because I had seen his picture. Christmas cards could not lie, they were the homely messages from God himself."[2]

Sadly, most of the loving messages, signatures and addresses on old Christmas cards still to be found at antique shows, antiquarian bookshops and through the collecting network are forever stripped of such personal meaning. We wonder wistfully what "Auntie" or "Susan" were like, where they lived, whether they were happy. So it was a delight when Mamelok Press archivist Kathleen Banks contributed turn-of-the-century holiday postcards from her family scrapbook and shared the story of the little girl to whom they were addressed so long ago. The cards, which include a delightful Father Christmas greeting published by Raphael Tuck, were sent to Elizabeth Annie (nicknamed Barbara) Knownas, who was born and raised in a Victorian cottage at Playford Brook, near Ipswich. Mrs. Banks writes: "To complete the picture, here is a photograph of the cottage at Playford Brook. The left-hand side of the pair of cottages at the top of the picture was home to the then little girl the cards were sent to. Two rooms up, two down and a kitchen." Imagine the excitement when the postman, in his bright red jacket, knocked at the door one chilly December day in 1905 and 1906 to hand Elizabeth Annie the cards pictured here — two Father Christmases and a pair of transformation cards whose hidden angels appeared "by magic," the same publisher's trick that had captivated Alison Uttley's young imagination a quarter of a century earlier.

Holiday postcard Santas, Befanas, Pelsnickles and Father Christmases crowd down the years, survivors from the past hung round with the romance of history, art and legend. They are a nostalgic touchpoint with yesterday and a ready design source for today's Santa doll artists. Equally inspiring are the wealth of surviving chromolithographed die-cuts many consider the ultimate distillation of pure Victoriana. Such paper scraps have their own tale to tell and deserve a chapter of their own.

[1] The History of The Christmas Card by George Buday (London, Spring Books, 1954), page 5.
[2] Country Things by Alison Uttley (London, Faber and Faber, 1946), pages 30-31.

A magnificent Christmas postcard postmarked 1903, from France. Papa Noël, in a hooded robe and wooden "sabots," carries the traditional grape basket loaded with evergreens, dolls and toys. *Photograph by Peter Groesbeck. Courtesy of Lois Clarkson.*

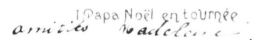

Christmas greetings, 1905 and 1907, received at Playford Brook by little Elizabeth Annie Knownas and preserved in her daughter-in-law's family album. *Photograph by Peter Groesbeck. Courtesy of Kathleen Banks.*

Christmas Greetings.

ABOVE LEFT: A village postman delivered this gorgeous Raphael Tuck Christmas postcard to Elizabeth Annie Knownas' cottage at Playford Brook in 1905. *Photograph by Peter Groesbeck. Courtesy of Kathleen Banks.*

ABOVE RIGHT: Another postcard, circa 1905, printed in Germany and marketed in England, from the family album of Mamelok Press' archivist, Kathleen Banks. *Photograph by Peter Groesbeck. Courtesy of Kathleen Banks.*

If you would see an Angel bright
Hold up this Card against the light.

Elizabeth Annie Knownas with her parents — the little girl who received the old holiday cards in the family album of Mamelok Press archivist, Kathleen Banks. *Photograph by Peter Groesbeck. Courtesy of Kathleen Banks.*

Elizabeth Annie's cottage at Playford Brook. Imagine the excitement when that long-ago postman knocked with his annual load of holiday greetings. The Knownases lived in the left-hand side of the pair of cottages at the top of the photograph. "Two rooms up, two down, and a kitchen." *Photograph courtesy of Kathleen Banks.*

If you would see two Angels bright
Hold up this Card against the light.

OPPOSITE PAGE and ABOVE: Transformation cards, like those described by Alison Uttley in *Country Things*. When Mrs. Uttley's favorite Christmas postcard was held against the light, Santa Claus materialized! Elizabeth Annie's transformation cards reveal lovely, and very Victorian, angels. *Photograph by Peter Groesbeck. Courtesy of Kathleen Banks.*

A 1908 "Printed in Germany" postcard marketed in the United States. A frail Father Christmas bows beneath a basket loaded with holiday toys, good luck gingerbread hearts, apples and the traditional switches. How sharp the contrast with the youthful Christ Child riding the donkey. *Photograph by Peter Groesbeck. Courtesy of Lois Clarkson.*

A sturdy, brown-robed Santa, just emerged from an old-world pine forest, shoulders a fresh-cut evergreen. Contemporary artists, like Lois Clarkson, Roberta ("Bobbie") Taylor and Rosemary Volpi, consider antique postcard Santas a major resource when developing their studio art. *Photograph by Peter Groesbeck. Courtesy of Lois Clarkson.*

A "Made in Germany" Christmas postcard mailed in Maryland and post-marked "December 1910." Artist Lois Clarkson calls this Santa a transitional type whose face, whiskers and red robe hint at the figure we love today, but whose cap, the cut of the costume and romantic Ludwig of Bavaria sleigh, belie his old-world roots. *Photograph by Peter Groesbeck. Courtesy of Lois Clarkson.*

RIGHT: A postcard greeting mailed from Germany to Chicago in 1912 features an old style, hooded Father Christmas whose looks clearly belie his well-preserved muscles (that's quite a tree!). Santa skis south from the Pole to gladden children's holidays everywhere. *Photograph by Peter Groesbeck. Courtesy of Dorothy Hesner.*

Father Christmas makes Christmas Presents.

To Wish You A Merry Christmas.

ABOVE: Rare American teddy bear Santa greeting with "Copyright 1907 Tanner Souvenir Co." printed on the face of the postcard. *From the collection of Susan Brown Nicholson.*

ABOVE RIGHT: An utterly delightful cat Santa designed by turn-of-the-century British artist Louis Wain, whose output included designs for humorous animal postcards. *From the collection of Susan Brown Nicholson.*

Saint Nicolas

A marvelous composite "Saint Nick" in a brown robe and hood combines features of the German Pelsnickle, Gift Givers and Old Man Winter. His sack is a mess, but his manners are exquisite. No chimney for this fellow; he rings the front doorbell! *From the collection of Susan Brown Nicholson.*

FAR LEFT: Father Christmas in fur-trimmed blue robe, thick peasant boots and fur hat, confers with the Christmas Angel, unaware of his juvenile observers. A French basket replaces the familiar sack. We count four evergreen stumps in the picture, martyrs to the holiday season. *From the collection of Susan Brown Nicholson.*

Perhaps the most charming postcard Father Christmas we know, this stout gentleman wears a brick red hood and free-flowing wool tunic in the mood of peasant smocks. He carries a sack, an oak walking stick and a fully-decorated evergreen. *From the collection of Susan Brown Nicholson.*

FAR LEFT: A regal and imposing Father Christmas postcard. The figure wears a glorious gold-stamped green velvet coat, fur-trimmed cap and knickers. He packs fruit, fancy toys and a charming doll, and his "swank" outfit includes, of all things, spats! *From the collection of Susan Brown Nicholson.*

Another regal Father Christmas from the same German publisher's Series 980 as Illustration on far left. Some of the gold-stamped motifs echo popular holiday cookie shapes. The card pictured was used in 1907, proof that it was issued in that year or earlier. Dating antique postcards is a very difficult business we were told by collector Susan Brown Nicholson. *From the collection of Susan Brown Nicholson.*

A charming composite of symbols. The gentleman wears monkish robes and a holly crown bedecked with toys and colorful ornaments. The Christmas robin, subject of innumerable Christian folk tales, perches on his shoulder. *From the collection of Susan Brown Nicholson.*

FAR RIGHT: According to expert Susan Brown Nicholson, this Uncle Sam, hold-to-the-light Santa postcard is the world's rarest and sells for over $1000 in today's collector marketplace. Compare it to the top right Illustration on page 22. Clearly a variant of the same master design. Publishers often dressed their Santas to suit local markets! *From the collection of Susan Brown Nicholson.*

A Thomas Nast size jolly old elf costumed *à l'européene.* Our son's comment: "Wow! What whiskers!" *From the collection of Susan Brown Nicholson.*

FAR RIGHT: This Saint Nicholas in Bishop's robe and miter was a common pre-World War I Christmas postcard design, according to Susan Brown Nicholson. Note that the Saint bears a sack of holiday toys in one hand and blesses little children with the other. *From the collection of Susan Brown Nicholson.*

Victorian Santa Scraps

Photographs by Peter Groesbeck

This heavily embossed, magnificent white-robed Father Christmas scenic, 9in (25cm) high, is a prize in any collection. Fifteen years ago, before scraps were "discovered" by collectors, this treasure was purchased for $2.50! *Photograph courtesy of Dorothy Hesner.*

This Santa twosome is as rare as it is charming, since it retains the critical tabs that identify the manufacturer, along with the notation "Printed in Germany." Sheets with this motif were issued in many sizes by Littauer and Boysen of Berlin. Santas pictured here are 2¼in (8cm) tall. *Photograph courtesy of Dorothy Hesner.*

LEFT: St. Nicholas wears his traditional bishop's robes in this elegant die-cut. The manufacturer is unknown although Illinois collector/dealer Dorothy Hesner is sure the piece was published in Germany. Twenty years ago, *four* of these 3¼in (8cm) die-cuts were purchased for 35 cents! *Photograph courtesy of Dorothy Hesner.*

With the advent of chromolithography in 1837, the Victorian middle classes stepped through the rainbow into a world drenched with color. For millions who had lived for centuries with somber black-and-white bookplates, broadsides, advertising art, books, magazines, stationery, letterheads and playing cards, where an overlay of color laboriously applied by hand doubled the cost to the consumer, affordable color transformed the world.

Full-color printed die-cuts called "scraps" or "chromos" were a side benefit of the printing revolution that changed Victorian society. The public became drunk on scraps poured into France, Britain and America by over 200 German publishing houses, and this ephemeral art form, originally designed as decorative paste-ons for German holiday cookies, quickly became a hobby craze Victorian style, which in that age of "do-dads" and whatnots meant home crafting on a giant scale. The cost of the hobby posed no problem. Scraps were cheap and became cheaper over time, when increased automation in factories reduced publishers' overhead expenses, a saving they passed along to the consumer. Well-known authority Francine Kirsch writes: "An 1894 article says that when scraps made their appearance in 1850s England, they sold at 80 shillings per 100 sheets. The same number of sheets could be purchased for *one* shilling forty years later...In general, chromos sold (at retail) for from 3 cents to 15 cents a sheet."[1]

Once purchased, the Victorians filled endless albums with these charming bits of paper. They made them into lace-backed bookmarks and gilt-edged greeting cards, used them as components for elaborate holiday ornaments, to cover boxes and screens, to decorate mirrors and picture frames and, in short, to provide endless hours of craft pleasure for women and children in the rainbow years that succeeded centuries of gloomy black-and-white printing.

There were paper cabbage roses, violets, black-eyed Susans and lush mixed bunches; scrap children in sailor suits, pinafores, Lord Fauntleroy costumes and Kate Greenaway dresses. There were exotic ladies with black lace mantillas and wild southern eyes, swashbuckling musketeers and whiskery sea captains, romantic castles, instructive nursery sets (ABCs, flower, animal and insect sheets), and commemoratives, — of World's Fairs, military triumphs, triumphs of progress (blimps, motor cars and the railroad), and a succulent feast for the eye to satisfy every holiday need. This included a wealth of Father Christmases to paste into albums, make into

An oversize piece, 7½in (19cm) tall, combines features of the die-cut and the paper doll. Like hundreds of similar scraps, this Santa is complete to the waist; it was left for the purchaser to craft the skirt for his robe, then attach die-cut boots. Surviving examples of similar hybrids wear robes of crepe paper, fabric, even spun glass. *Photograph courtesy of Dorothy Hesner.*

A beautiful partial sheet of nickel-sized Father Christmas heads, *circa* 1890. Original publisher unidentified. *Photograph courtesy of Dorothy Hesner.*

tree ornaments, glue up as greeting cards or simply to hoard in boxes.

Among survivors of this mob of Santas are every permutation and interpretation of Old Claus familiar to our ancestors. There are mitered Bishops (in The Netherlands, equestrian "Saint Nicholas" still rides through the streets of Amsterdam in full Bishop's regalia every 5th of December), dour Pelsnickles from Germany with fir trees slung across their shoulders, bright, mica-flecked angels and idealized angel children with magic wings mysteriously hooked to the backs of fur-trimmed couturier wool coats. We find the Christkind, that mysterious bearer of gifts, barefoot and dressed in filmy white. There are blue-robed, hooded French Père Noëls. There are bent figures of Old Man Winter creeping through the bracken clutching rough oaken staffs. And there are Baccanalian Spirits of The Christmas Feast decked in holly crowns and brandishing giant plum puddings. Saint Nicholas appears, both alone and with children, lugging satchels, spilling the contents of baskets onto snow-blanketed forest floors, and swinging brown sacks bulging with holiday toys. He wears white, blue, gray, brown, red or green robes, and comes booted, sabot'd, slippered or barefoot, hooded, wreathed or

crowned. We find him morose or smiling, tall or short, lean or stout. The old designers were attentive to detail and concerned that their compositions be consistent. Mamelok Press archivist Kathleen Banks has noted that when children pictured in a Father Christmas scenic scrap are dressed poorly, Santa's sack holds oranges, apples, nuts and other holiday eatables. When the children are richly apparelled, the sack overflows with luxury toys, dolls and extravagantly illustrated picture books in luxury bindings.

For Christmas collectors, paper doll enthusiasts who include scraps as a sub-collection within the larger hobby and for doll artists seeking authentic period sources to use as a base for contemporary Santa art, scraps provide an unequalled resource mill. This, despite the fact that antique examples are hard to come by nowadays and prices for those that have survived damp cellars, dry attics, mice and war have long since outstripped the purses of most collectors. Fortunately, revival of interest in all things Victorian has brought forth a bonanza of recent books aglow with reprinted scraps, many of which are Christmas related. And antique scrap reproductions that include fabulous Santas at reasonable prices are available from at least one publisher, who has main-

A very secular late 19th century Spirit of Christmas scrap, 6¾in (17cm) tall. Toys tumbling from the basket include balls and tops, a dollhouse, dolls, a sword, watch, plum pudding and a book titled *Christmas. Photograph courtesy of Mamelok Press Ltd.*

Old-world Father Christmas scraps designed and printed in Germany for the late Victorian English market. Figures wear the hood, long robes and solemn demeanor that predate the jolly face universalized by Thomas Nast. *Photograph courtesy of Mamelok Press Ltd.*

tained continuous production for over 150 years, despite changing patterns within the marketplace and the chaos of two World Wars. The firm is Mamelok Press, established in Breslau in 1827 and still owned by the founder's family in 1990.

From the beginning, Mamelok & Söhne produced top-quality scraps and was among the leaders in the field. Then, in the 1920s, the popularity of scraps decreased substantially, and vast numbers of established publishers were forced to shut down their presses. The reason was a shift in the public's leisure time activities pattern. "The demand for scraps fell as people stopped creating their own entertainment." we read in Alistair Allen and Joan Hoverstadt's *The History of Printed Scraps.* "Radio and the cinema drew interest away from craft work and homemade pastimes. When Scrap Books were kept they took on a different 'look'. Pages could be cut from magazines, comics, colored advertising plates or women's journals. Albums were not kept as treasured books, but more as recreational time fillers, and they were more readily thrown away. For a fast consumer society, in which values and tastes had changed, the traditional scrap was no longer relevant although scraps had brought many hours of joy to both children and adults during the past 150 years."[2]

Despite the downward trend in sales and popularity during the 1920s, Mamelok continued scraps production and even expanded its holdings by purchasing stock, plates and equipment from former competitors. Then, in the 1930s, the family-owned business confronted the social upheaval that preceded World War II, and owner Arthur Mamelok, his wife, Cecily, and their children left Germany to resettle in England. After a sojourn in London, the firm moved to its present quarters in Bury St. Edmunds, Suffolk. Amazingly, the Mameloks were able to transport much of their workshop tool kit and machinery, valuable antique plates and priceless sample books, some dating to the early 19th century, to their new home in the United Kingdom.

Today, Mamelok Press publishes new scrap sheets that appeal to modern youngsters and also reprints antique sheets from precious archival plates. The firm's antique repros include dozens of vintage Santas with tremendous appeal to nostalgia buffs, craft hobbyists and collectors and, like the Christmas postcard of the same era, scraps have become a prime inspirational source for today's Santa doll artist.

[1] *Cf. Chromos* (A.S. Barnes & Company, 1981), pages 39 and 43.
[2] Op. Cit., page 32.

ABOVE LEFT: Vintage scraps demonstrate Santa's emerging image. Shown are two grim, hooded early 19th century types, a transitional St. Nick (bottom left) and a plump, rosy fellow that almost, but not quite, fits the 20th century stereotype. He lacks the twinkle and still sports hood and holly. *Photograph courtesy of Mamelok Press Ltd.*

ABOVE RIGHT: A powerful Spirit of Christmas figure published in Germany for the turn-of-the-century English market. This impressive old gentleman combines qualities of the Gift Bearer and the Winter-of-Life symbol. Note his stooped shoulders, careworn face and the cane. *Photograph courtesy of Mamelok Press Ltd.*

Three Spirits of Christmas Past. Note the elephant in the satchel (top right), a toy popularized when Jumbo, the giant pachyderm, was sold by the London Zoo to P.T. Barnum amid storm and scandal in 1882. *Photograph courtesy of Mamelok Press Ltd.*

Father Christmases pose with typically angelic scraps children. With child mortality statistics appallingly high in all ranks of Victorian society, print makers, illustrators, authors and scraps publishers capitalized on sentimentality born of fear. They depicted childhood as a safe world aglow with health and laughter, a paradise unblemished by danger, poverty or disease. *Photograph courtesy of Mamelok Press Ltd.*

Uncut sample sheet from Mamelok's archives. The largest of the early 20th century Santas pictured is an impressive 13in (33cm) tall. *Photograph courtesy of Mamelok Press Ltd.*

A page from Mamelok's circa 1900-1920 archival albums with designs for an equestrian St. Nicholas in the Dutch mood. The group was available in two sizes, with St. Nick astride a white horse or a donkey. The handwritten note explains that *large* sheets in this design included 18 motifs, *smaller* sheets 40. *Photograph courtesy of Mamelok Press Ltd.*

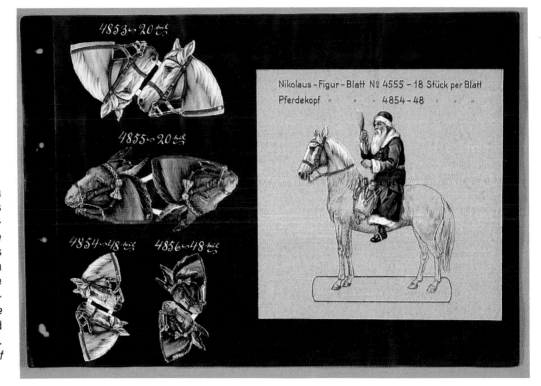

Father Christmases from the early 1900s. The Santa at the right is 12½in (32cm) tall and carries a clown, doll and a German/Prussian Nutcracker dressed as a soldier. *Photograph courtesy of Mamelok Press Ltd.*

"Fancy" Santas! Four pre-1930 Christmas Wizards published by Mamelok & Söhne. Figures average 4¾in (12cm) tall. *Photograph courtesy of Mamelok Press Ltd.*

Rare blue-hooded German Santa head. This scrap echoes both the benevolent Father Christmas and the wild Christmas Man. *Photograph courtesy of Mamelok Press Ltd.*

Four pre-1930 German Santas, publisher unknown. Dating clues, according to Mamelok Press archivist Kathleen Banks, include the toy airplane and tinplate Brooklands-type car in the center sacks. *Photograph courtesy of Mamelok Press Ltd.*

A good luck train, circa 1930, with "Guess Who" at the throttle! This holiday scrap is 3¼in (8cm) wide. *Photograph courtesy of Mamelok Press Ltd.*

BELOW: An east European driver in a primitive sleigh pulled by a reindeer. The reindeer has been the beast of burden in the north for centuries but only fused with the emerging American Santa tradition in 1821, when a best-selling juvenile book, *The Children's Friend*, was published in New York City. One color plate depicts "Santeclaus" (sic) driving a sleigh pulled by a single reindeer. *Photograph courtesy of Mamelok Press Ltd.*

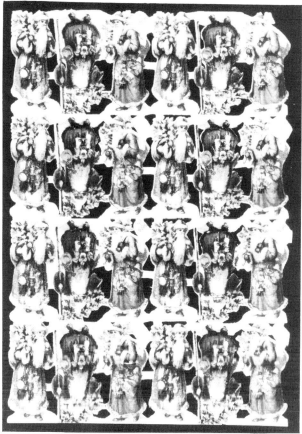

Rare, uncut sheet in pristine condition. The old publisher neglected to print his firm's logo in the connecting tabs, hence, he cannot be identified. *Photograph courtesy of Mamelok Press Ltd.*

LEFT: Bells and holly and a late-19th-century Father Christmas peeking through a cheery holiday wreath 4in (10cm) high. *Photograph courtesy of Mamelok Press Ltd.*

Assorted old-style hooded Father Christmases from Germany combine the benignity of the venerable Saint with the holly wreath of the Christmas Man. Hoods are blue, red, green and brown. *Photograph courtesy of Dorothy Hesner.*

Four grim red-, blue- and raspberry-robed Father Christmases from a century ago. Note the posture of the figures and the presence of saddles and stirrups. Surely there once was a companion sheet filled with elegant horses or sturdy donkeys. *Photograph courtesy of Mamelok Press Ltd.*

A beautiful Littauer and Boysen fragment depicts St. Nicholas wearing the traditional bishop's miter. The old designer used poetic license to color miters alternately red and green. Each head is 3¾in (10cm) high. *Photograph courtesy of Dorothy Hesner.*

LEFT: Two die-cuts from a large sheet published by Littauer and Boysen of Berlin (they were bought out by Mamelok & Söhne in 1920). Each old-style figure doubles as a paper doll for which the purchaser added a skirt to complete Santa's robe. *Photograph courtesy of Dorothy Hesner.*

Antique Father Christmas Dolls, Toys and Oddments

Years ago, during an art history lecture, the professor pulled a bronze 15th-century icon from his pocket and passed it down the rows of students. "Feel it," he said. "Turn it over and over in your hands. Absorb the texture, the weight, the smell, the warmth of the metal. Handling the real thing is the only way to gain complete understanding of a work of art."

He was right, of course. Which is why, although paper memorabilia — faded letters, holiday postcards, antique advertising art — may fascinate by its beauty as well as its history, it cannot thrill us as deeply as do actual artifacts, the rubbed, chipped, three-dimensional survivors of Old Christmas. They are the stuff that Christmas Past was actually made of — the very dolls, toys and oddments that transformed shops, arcades, parlors and nurseries into joyous dreams to treasure throughout a lifetime a century or more ago.

Standing tall among these playthings from the past, at center stage or in the wings, is Father Christmas himself, rendered in card, in tin, in cast iron, in wood, china or papier-mâché. There are German glass and cotton batting tree Santas, early 20th century celluloid, rubber and cloth-faced Santas, molded Belsnickles with mica chips still sparkling on timeworn painted surfaces. The examples pictured here include classic types shown again and again in toy histories and in the gorgeously illustrated holiday issues of art and collector magazines. Also included are unusual, one-of-a-kind pieces, some with and some forever separated from their fantastic histories.

Commercially manufactured antique Santas include cottage industry products like the old papier-mâché or pressed paper molded Belsnickles from Germany, each hand cast, hand-painted and enhanced with sparkling flecks of applied mica. These images of dour traditional German Christmas Men are being reproduced today by descendants of the original makers and, working from old chocolate and ice cream molds of similar design, Vaillancourt Folk Art® of Sutton, Massachusetts, has created a line of stunning repros of 19th century display figures. Notice how closely the cast iron Santa bank, made circa 1895-1910 by the Hubley Company of Lancaster, Pennsylvania, and included among our illustrations, resembles contemporary molded Belsnickles from Europe. With Lancaster at the heart

of Pennsylvania German country, it is reasonable to find the old-world images preserved in local craft work.

Another group of classic, commercially manufactured German Santas being reproduced today (*Cf.* our "Lew Kummerow" chapter), — same methods, same materials — are Father Christmas candy containers, those delightful rabbit-fur-whiskered, red-felt-clad Santas, some protruding from wide brick paper chimneys, some seated in sleighs or wagons made of sticks from Bavarian forests, some standing alone. In *Christmas Past*, author Robert Brenner tells how these 1880s-early 1900s figures, along with other holiday-related shaped candy containers, were made to be filled and hung on the Christmas tree. "The great majority of these," he writes, "were originally given to youngsters as gifts from Sunday school teachers, from churches on Christmas Eve, and from school teachers as part of Christmas festivities." Mr. Brenner adds that such figures, in various sizes, were advertised in Butler Brothers' catalogs for 1889 and 1903. In 1889, three sizes were offered. "The five cent figure represented old Kris Kringle in snow-covered 'garb in which he has always been pictured to Children.' This figure is shown as carrying an evergreen tree with colored ornaments. He was five inches (13cm) in height and decorated with gold tinsel to represent the sparkling snow. The next size offered was 7½ inches (19cm) high and was to be sold for ten cents. He also carries an evergreen tree, but this tree was decorated with berries. He had a finely painted red face and white beard, and was dressed in a heavy coat covered with gold tinsel. He was made hollow so that he could be used as a candy box. The third size offered was 11 inches (28cm) high and meant to sell for twenty-five cents. This figure was also made hollow so that it could be used as a confectionery box. The head was bound in chenille to imitate fur and the coat was sprinkled with gold spangles. This papier-mâché figure also carried an evergreen tree with berries."[1]

Some commercially manufactured Santas are among the rarest and most highly valued of antique toys in the collecting world. Heading the list, surely, is Althof Bergmann's gorgeous Father Christmas-in-Sleigh with goats bell toy, of which only two or three examples have survived. One of these is in the

Homemade 19th-century American Belsnickle, probably from Pennsylvania. Note the switches, florid face and savage mouth, features a world removed from the benevolent Santa of today. *Photograph courtesy of The Colonial Williamsburg Foundation. Williamsburg, Virginia.*

Carved and painted Santa Claus (1875-1900) attributed to American artist Charles Robb. For 40 years this figure belonged to a Lutheran church on New York's Bleecker Street. *Photograph courtesy of The Colonial Williamsburg Foundation. Williamsburg, Virginia.*

permanent collection of the Margaret Woodbury Strong Museum in Rochester, New York. Another, formerly in the Barenholtz Collection, sold at auction recently for $75,000. In 1990, California artist Lew Kummerow reproduced this toy as a gorgeous, one-of-a-kind piece. The "repro" is pictured in the chapter about Lew's work.

Among the more amusing commercially produced Santas from the 1890s is Ives' cast iron walking Santa Claus where the patented movement was designed by Arthur Hotchkiss of Cheshire, Connecticut, in 1875. Ives fitted an interesting group of character dolls with the Hotchkiss mechanism, and surviving figures include the Empress Eugénie, a Turk, a Chinaman, a jackass (probably a spinoff of a familiar Thomas Nast political cartoon series), "Tilden The Statesman," and "Old Black Joe," in addition to Santa

Claus. In *American Clockwork Toys*, authority Blair Whitton tells how the legs of each of these figures attach to oversize cast iron shoes that conceal free-turning wooden rollers on the underside. "The legs have an alternating back and forth movement and with the help of the rollers provide an adequate walking motion."[2]

Apart from commercially made and marketed toys in tin, wood, papier-mâché and cast iron, there were delightful cloth Santas and now-rare novelty paper dolls, lightweight Santa and Christmas tree folders that open to reveal pockets crammed with delightful paper dolls, dolls' clothes and accessories. Of old cloth doll survivors, possibly the most charming are the 15in (38cm) figures with two front sides designed in 1884-1886 by Edward S. Peck of Brooklyn, New York. Peck held the patent, but the textile

Rare fur-clad German Knecht Ruprecht given by Queen Victoria to a little English girl at Christmas, 1885. The original owner presented the doll to The Lilliput Museum on the Isle of Wight nearly a century later. *Photograph courtesy of The Lilliput Museum of Antique Dolls and Toys, Brading, Isle of Wight, United Kingdom.*

Ives' Walking Santa Claus, one in a circa 1890 series that included a walking Turk, Empress Eugénie, Uncle Tom and a jackass! A clockwork movement causes the legs to move; the figure rolls forward on wooden spools concealed beneath cast iron shoes. *Photograph courtesy of David Bausch, Allentown, Pennsylvania.*

was printed at The Oriental Print Works, then sold by the New York Stationery and Envelope Company. It is thought that these dolls inspired the rag doll art of Celia and Charity Smith.

The list is endless. Santa dolls were issued by Simon & Halbig, Heubach, Lenci, and Steiff, by the J. & E. Stevens Company, Kyser & Rex, by "snow baby" manufacturers and by the Rushton Company (now defunct) of Atlanta, Georgia, which was commissioned to produce Coca-Cola® Santas in conjunction with Coca-Cola's enormously successful Christmas advertising campaign during the 1930s-1950s.

Curious indeed are the one-of-a-kind Santas that have come down the years. Survivors include a very German Belsnickle, almost certainly homemade in western Pennsylvania, a papier-mâché figure with

aqua coat and hat trimmed with white fleece. This diabolical character clutches a linen bag from which protrudes the head of a frightened child. Far gentler (and far better art!) is a treasured carved and painted wood Santa Claus made between 1875-1900, now in the permanent collection of the Abby Aldrich Rockefeller Folk Art Center in Williamsburg, Virginia. For 40 years, this piece, probably the work of Charles Robb, a top-ranking American carver of trade figures and circus wagons, graced a Lutheran Church on New York's Bleecker Street.

Unique relics include marionettes and hand puppets, home-crafted carved wood toys, cloth and papier-mâché figures, store display pieces (many automated) and commercially-manufactured dolls that have been charmingly home costumed in Santa suits for the holidays.

Delightfully-eccentric cloth Santa, probably late 19th century. Lost forever is the tale behind this marvelous doll with his Russian moujik jacket and exotic air. *Photograph courtesy of Swanson's Auctions, Mountain Center, California.*

Painted cast iron Santa bank (1895-1910) by Hubley of Lancaster, Pennsylvania. The design echoes European Belsnickles and 19th century German chocolate mold figures. *Photograph courtesy of The Colonial Williamsburg Foundation, Williamsburg, Virginia.*

Edward S. Peck's double-fronted 1884-1886 cloth Santas. The whimsical dolls are each 15in (38cm) tall. *Photograph courtesy of The Colonial Williamsburg Foundation, Williamsburg, Virginia.*

A 1903 Belfast studio portrait of children's author and inventor of *The Chronicles of Narnia* C.S. Lewis, then aged five, with his favorite toy, a German Father Christmas mounted on a donkey. Might the heroic role played by Father Christmas in the Narnian adventures be an echo of nursery days and ways? *Copyright The Marion E. Wade Center, Wheaton College, Wheaton, Illinois, USA.*

From California comes this fragile, highly-collectible Tiffany glass Santa dating from 1915. The piece is 10in (25cm) high. *Photograph courtesy of Butterfield and Butterfield, San Francisco, California.*

Late 19th and early 20th century Santas pictured include a composition head Father Christmas in original clothes, a circa 1920/1930 jointed composition Santa and an 11½in (29cm) circa 1930 celluloid and composition Father Christmas from Japan. This clockwork figure plays a drum and moves his head realistically. At right, a composition candy container with clockwork nodding head. *Photograph courtesy of Christie's Colour Library, London, England.*

Christmas stock dominates the 1906 showrooms of George Borgfeldt, a major commission buying agent for the German toy trade, with offices in New York City, Vienna, Berlin and Sonneberg (Thuringia). By the 1920s, the firm transacted about $27 million worth of business annually. *Photograph courtesy of Daniel Shackman Jacoby. Antique Toy World Magazine, Nov. 1990, Vol 20, Nº 11.*

Possibly the most extraordinary Christmas doll of all is a small bisque fur-clad Knecht Ruprecht we learned about from British friend Ann Parker. The doll, a treasure in the collection of The Lilliput Museum of Antique Dolls and Toys on Britain's Isle of Wight, came to the museum with its history complete. Margaret Whitaker, museum founder and director, explained that this doll is very special for two reasons. "It is known as Knecht Ruprecht and is of German origin, and it represents an animal (in this case a dog) which played a significant role in the German Christmas celebration. In old Germany, the role of Knecht Ruprecht was played by one of the household servants who put on an animal disguise just before Christmas and visited the family parlor when the young children were present. If the children had been good and had thought of Christmas

and the Christ Child in the religious context as opposed to the more commercial aspect of the holiday, Ruprecht would reward them with sweets, apples and nuts. If they had been naughty, he would chastise them with the rod he carried. He was an awesome and frightening figure.

"Our Knecht Ruprecht doll at the museum is very rare," Mrs. Whitaker continued, "especially as it is of excellent quality and condition. It was presented by Queen Victoria herself, at a Christmas party at Osborne House here on the Isle of Wight, to a little guest, the daughter of an estate employee, in 1885. The 'little girl' sent me the doll when she was ninety-three years of age with the request that I look after it and treasure it as she had, and this we are honored to do."

Today's Santa artists draw on this vast well of Father Christmas art from the past. And, of course, they are influenced by the spirit and culture of the times they themselves live in. Couple these factors with first rate talent, vastly varied and highly individual studio philosophies and techniques, and it is no wonder Santa doll crafting has become an exciting art form in the 1990s.

[1] Robert Brenner, *Christmas Past* (West Chester, PA, Schiffer Publishing Ltd., 1985), page 32.
[2] Blair Whitton, *American Clockwork Toys, 1862-1900* (Westchester, PA, Schiffer Publishing Ltd., 1981), page 90.

Rare antique card folders contain charming holiday paper dolls and accessories. Such Christmas novelties were common early in the century. All three pictured are from the same (unknown) German publisher. *Photograph by Peter Groesbeck. Courtesy of Margaret Whitton.*

The blue Father Christmas paper doll folder, opened, contains a little girl with teddy bear, a "life-size" teddy bear costume, toys and a paper period wardrobe. *Photograph by Peter Groesbeck. Courtesy of Margaret Whitton.*

Early 20th century group. A German doll with sensational whiskers; a Rushton Coca-Cola® Santa Claus and Steiff's 1953 replica of their classic 11½in (29cm) rubber-faced Santa with jointed head, arms and legs, mohair beard, felt body and felt clothes. Photograph courtesy of Swanson's Auctions, Mountain Center, California.

Early 20th century Santa Claus and elf puppets. Fully-articulated papier-mâché bodies with reinforced wire joints, painted faces, mohair wigs and whiskers and handmade clothes. Santa is 36in (91cm) tall. Elves average 20in (51cm). *Photograph courtesy of Swanson's Auctions, Mountain Center, California.*

Antique or contemporary — a puzzler when faced with this 10in (25cm) papier-mâché Belsnickle cast from a turn-of-the-century mold by descendants of the original craftsman. Made in Germany's Neustadt Valley, Belsnickle reissues are hand-painted, aged and signed works indistinguishable from antique pieces except by chemical testing. The piece pictured, made by the Schaller family in 1990, holds a goose feather branch tipped with a "holly berry." *Photograph by Peter Groesbeck. Courtesy of Pine Tree Enterprises.*

Trio of antique Santas. A papier-mâché American figure, circa 1940; a mica-sprinkled papier-mâché German Belsnickle, circa 1890-1910 and a pre-1900 German Father Christmas wearing felt clothes with papier-mâché face and rabbit fur beard. Belsnickle is 11¼in (29cm) tall. *Photograph courtesy of Le Château Interiors.*

Christmas magic! Antique Santas from Germany and Japan, a holiday tree smothered with handblown glass ornaments, one candle... *Photograph courtesy of Le Château Interiors.*

Early 20th century celluloid Santas. The largest measures 7in (18cm) tall. *Photograph courtesy of Le Château Interiors.*

Early 20th century German, Japanese and Mexican Santas in a wide range of sizes and styles. The rare Mexican figure is in the back row with a low hood and a cross. *Photograph courtesy of Le Château Interiors.*

Assorted Santas, 1910-1940. Santas in white sleigh and next to chimney are Japanese, circa 1930. Fat papier-mâché Santa with sack is American, circa 1940. Others are candy containers from Germany and Japan. *Photograph courtesy of Le Château Interiors.*

A circa 1930 Coca-Cola® Santa Claus manufactured by the Rushton Company (now out-of-business) for Coca-Cola's popular 1930s-1950s advertising campaign. Santa's companion is a Rushton clown. *Photograph courtesy of Barbara Spears, Barbara's Dolls, Fort Worth, Texas.*

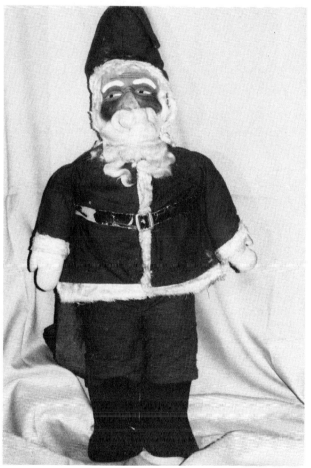

Circa 1930 molded face cloth Santa stuffed with cotton. This Christmas Man measures 26in (66cm) from the soles of his boots to the peak of his cap. His sack contains an early 1900s cloth doll and an early teddy. *Photograph courtesy of Barbara Spears, Barbara's Dolls, Fort Worth, Texas.*

Electrically-powered Santa from the late 1930s. This fellow is 46in (116cm) tall and wears red velvet with white plush cuffs. Plug him in and push the switch! His left arm waves and he bows from the hips. The figure was probably a show window display piece. *Photograph courtesy of Butterfield and Butterfield, San Francisco, California.*

Father Christmas Doll Makers Today
(Introduction)

Molded felt dolls from the studio of R. John Wright include this appealing duo. At left: a Saint Nicholas in the Steiff character doll tradition, made in the early 1970s. At right: a 1979 "Spirit of Christmas," elegant in hooded robe over a felt tunic and sash. *Photograph courtesy of The Enchanted Doll House, Manchester Center, Vermont.*

There isn't a book thick enough to contain in-depth profiles of every first-rate Santa craftsperson at work in the United States today. The profusion of gorgeous dolls and display figures and the near-infinite variety of materials and inspirational sources for these beautiful pieces are mind-boggling. Artists carve Santas of wood and mold them in porcelain. Father Christmases are rag-over-wire, wax-over-wood, corn husk, papier-mâché, synthetic or natural clay and cloth. They come in every imaginable size, from 1in (3cm) tinies to 6ft (nearly 2m) giants. There are ethnic Santas, Tolkienesque wizard-of-the-woods Santas, Victorian Father Christmases, Coca-Cola® and purely imaginative Santas. Russian Father Frosts, German snow babies and Neapolitan crèche angels, Pelsnickles, Black Peters and mitered Bishops joined the fantastic crowd of Christmas figures pushing and jostling one another in an effort to climb into these pages. Choosing what to include was hard; deciding what to leave out (regretfully) was even harder. The answer, in the end, was to present an overview, a 1990s Santa sampler, followed by in-depth profiles of representative artists, some already household words among seasoned collectors, some assured household words of the future. By this means, we hope to convey some idea of the beauty, originality and very personal motivation that characterize Santa art today. Note that dollhouse Santas, Santa teddies and other, sometimes startling animal Santas have been assigned chapters of their own.

The "folk to fine art" range of artist doll Santa Clauses include work by celebrated cloth doll artist R. John Wright, whose Saint Nicholas in the mood of old Steiff character dolls was among John's earliest ventures into dolldom. That #1 Father Christmas was followed by others, including a 1979 Spirit of Christmas pictured here. Like more recent dolls from the artist's upstate New York studio, the 1979, 18in (46cm) limited edition Spirit of Christmas is hand-crafted of felt with a molded felt face and hand-painted features. His body is jointed to allow arms, legs and head to move realistically. The figure is elegantly costumed in a hooded red robe over a felt tunic, with long underwear and Bishop's shoes. Presently, the R. John Wright studio is designing a different and very elaborate Father Christmas, modelled after Arthur Rackham's famous illustrations for A Visit from Saint Nicholas. "This piece should be magnificent," a spokesperson for the studio told us.

Equally joyous but in a very different mood is Paula Watkins' Victorian 13in (33cm) Father Christmas, a 1980 special commission for the Louisiana collection of Frank Hanley and Jeffery Guéno. Paula's painted silk-over-composition figure carries a marvelous toy sack filled with old-fashioned toys she made herself. These include cloth and wooden dolls, an "antique" drum, tiny tin toys, a fully-jointed teddy bear and Mr. Punch.

Paula Watkins' Santa is exquisite and elegant; the "legendary Saint Nicks" made by Mary Alice Byerly of Grosse Pointe Woods, Michigan, bubble with fun and whimsy. This artist, whose background includes a lifelong passion for the arts and years of professional experience as an interior decorator, redirected her fabric, texture and Christmas interests early in 1989 to craft her #1 Saint Nicholas. Mary Alice has modified her original molded Santa head again and again, changing the expression and cast of the features while the clay is malleable greenware — then makes up beautifully costumed and accessorized editions of 100 which include humorous details like paired miniature bound books titled Boys and Girls, snowshoed Saint Nicks and at-home Santas dressed in crocheted slippers and cozy hand knit pullovers.

Past and present meet when contemporary artists try their hand at constructing an Old Father Christmas project originally published in Godey's Lady's Book in December 1868. For the Hanley/Guéno collection, artist "Susan" followed the 19th century instructions to produce a fabulous rendering of the faded drawing in the old magazine. Here are the prescribed five fir cones, the hair and beard of flax and a pack of artist crafted toys that echo those in Thomas Nast illustrations.

For collectors who wish to try this holiday project from the past, the Godey instructions follow:

"Many of our subscribers will be happy to copy the well-known figure on our illustration for their young darlings, and thus make Merry Christmas still merrier. This doll is principally composed of five fir cones. Two of them form the arms, two the legs, one the body. The boots, which are cut out of wood, are fastened upon a board, and are pointed off at the top. These points, two inches long, are inserted into the fir-cones which form the legs, after holes have been bored into the latter. The arms and legs are fastened on the body with gum and wire. The hands are made of papier-mâché, and are gummed on the arms. The head is also of papier-mâché, the hair and beard of flax. The doll has a waistband of moss to hide the wire. The neck and shoulders are covered with a black crocheted comforter, the head with a fur cap. The doll has, moreover, a basket of blue cardboard on the back, filled with confectionery and small toys; on the other shoulder a net filled with nuts and apples; in one hand a miniature Christmas tree; in the other a nutcracker and birch rod."

Inspired by Godey's, but oh so different are two pieces by Topeka, Kansas artist Barbara Kingman. "The Godey idea fascinated me," Barbara said, "but I wanted to breathe life into the original stiff figure. So I made Piney Woods Father Christmas, an elusive, shy magical Santa Claus. His costume is pure imagination spiced with Victoriana."

Barbara Kingman's prize-winning "Piney" was followed by her Sodbuster Santa, "a natural progression if you have a quirky mind like mine!" she explained. Sodbuster is a robust prairie Santa Claus with corncob legs and arms; he wears a blue denim tunic and a cherry red stocking cap. For each figure, Barbara sculpted a prototype head of thermal clay, then made a mold from which a limited edition of 100 was cast. Santa is fastened securely to carved wooden feet anchored to a rustic base cut from a cross section of tree branch with the bark intact. The 14in (36cm) dolls are dressed in new natural fiber fabrics or vintage materials. "They are meant to be whimsical, imaginative characters, to make us smile and remind us of the humble setting of the first Christmas," the artist said. "The worldly, materialistic excesses of today's celebrations are a poor substitute for the gifts of the spirit."

Yet one step closer to pure folk art are the droll cloth dolls made by Pennsylvania artist Judy Grocki. Some of Judy's small-scale personalities are products of her remarkably fertile imagination; others are spin-offs of old American or European designs. She works small, in a scale that approximates 1in (3cm) = 1ft (31cm), because "that's the size I can take with me and pull out anywhere — in the car, on a plane, at a football game, in the living room in the evening."

Judy makes rabbits for Easter, pumpkins and witches for Halloween, angels and Santas for Christmas, and collectors of her work are obsessive about it. She averages 30 new Santa designs every year, each a high-spirited variant of her amusing "signature figure."

Judy Grocki's tiny Santas have shoulder and hip joints made of strong thread anchored with beads. Bushy whiskers, hair and moustachios are sheep wool garnered from a flock that once roamed the family's rural Pennsylvania farm. "The only problem with my Santas," Judy confided, "is that they are thin men instead of fat men. Each is essentially a two-dimensional figure with a big belly that looks great in profile but disappears when viewed frontally. I want my Santas fat any way you look at them, so I'm anxious to solve the design problem."

The range of front rank art produced by Father Christmas craftspeople is staggering, as is obvious from the work described and pictured here. To complete the journey from fine art to folk art, enter the Tennessee studio of Johnny and Becky McGrew, whose deceptively naive looking roughly-carved white pine Santas resemble work by old German master carvers like Pennsylvania's Schimmel.

Until a few years ago, Johnny McGrew was a mill worker who carved his primitive wood sculptures after hours. Today, Johnny is a full-time artist who finds it hard to keep up with collectors' orders. The McGrews have a double studio focus, — carrousel animals (Johnny is active in the American Carrousel Association and the National Carrousel Association) — and Christmas sculptures.

Johnny and Becky make a "roly doll" Santa ("He can't get fatter than that!") and a Southern Santa dressed in gray with a carved pine Confederate flag in his basket. A grim Black Peter, with horns and a bundle of real switches in his basket, grasps a somber wooden book inscribed with the names of naughty children. The McGrews also craft a jointed pine Santa Claus available in large (1m) or mega (1⅔m) size. Each of the artists' sculptures is carved by Johnny, then painted by Becky. "It was hard to actually take the plunge and strike out on our own as free-lance artists," Becky told us, adding: "Not so any longer! We're doing well at what we love best, and collector letters we receive tell us we're putting our bit of fun into the holiday art world."

Speaking of fun, no overview would be complete without a bow from New Hampshire artist Maggie Anderson's one-of-a-kind 8½in (22cm) crocheted Santa Claus made in 1976, who actually flew cross-country to join our Christmas party! And the author's Christmas pal, the No-elf (a finger puppet by Folkmanis® of Emeryville, California), wishes it made clear that every word of this manuscript was personally supervised by himself. "I'm an Old-world type loose in the New World," the No-elf said with habitual bluntness, "so I'm your man to check out this kind of project and keep my writer friend on course!"

And he reminded us of the elaborate Father Christmas group assembled by Louisiana collectors/craftsmen Frank Hanley and Jeffery Guéno, a holiday romp that may well be the ultimate one-of-a-kind Christmas collectible. Its gifted creators are active UFDC members, juried Fellows of the International Guild of Miniature Artisans and noted collectors of antiques, dolls, miniatures and toys.

A number of years ago, Frank and Jeffery purchased a century-old salesman sample trunk with the original St. Louis manufacturer's label still pasted inside the lid. This stunning piece, with its elegant brasses, leather straps, working lock and rabbit warren of intriguing storage compartments, helped inspire an exciting project after the 1980 UFDC Convention. Together with a Convention "giveaway," a porcelain doll head made by Beverly Walter to represent a whiskery old gentleman, the trunk became the focus of a sensational composition.

"We decided to make up a fantasy setting that would depict the world's most famous traveler," Frank told us, "a Santa doll using the Beverly Walter doll head. We would fill the old St. Louis trunk to overflowing with an enormous wardrobe designed and sewn by Jeffery and myself, as well as with hundreds of appropriate antique accessories from our personal collection. We didn't know then that it would take years to finish that wardrobe, nor could we anticipate the stir the finished group would create in miniature and doll circles. Why, our 'traveler' hasn't stopped travelling since we made him! He has won

Godey's Lady's Book illustration showing the magazine's famous craft project completed. This Santa, be he made of fir cones, spruce cones or pine cones, has continued to inspire amateur and professional doll makers since the design was introduced in December 1868. *Photograph by Peter Groesbeck. Courtesy of Le Château Interiors.*

A contemporary Father Christmas by "Susan," crafted from directions in the December 1868 *Godey's Lady's Book*. Body is five fir cones; hair and beard are flax. Toys in Santa's pack are in the mood of Thomas Nast illustrations. *Photograph courtesy of Le Château Interiors.*

countless awards, Best of Shows and has been exhibited at numerous museums, including the Atlanta Toy Museum."

And no wonder! Frank and Jeffery's 18in (46cm) Santa Claus is an astonishing fellow. To begin with, he possesses two interchangeable bodies ("So we could dress a fat Santa *and* a thin one!"). The doll's original kit legs included black porcelain boots. These legs are removable and can be replaced by an alternate pair that accommodate the doll's luxury footwear — numerous pairs of boots and shoes, antique and modern slippers, even in-scale snowshoes. In Santa's extensive wardrobe, there are assorted robes and Santa Claus suits, undergarments (including long johns), handkerchiefs and a leather apron to wear in the workshop. Santa's "kit" includes antique and contemporary accessories that any well-dressed gentleman would welcome on his travels. He possesses shaving implements, a world globe, an American flag, a spirits can with a set of shot glasses, a complete lap desk ensemble, an antique Limoges porcelain tea set in its original leather carrying case and a bundle of switches. An antique compass is housed in an "antiqued" leather case made by Jeffery Guéno. There are assorted clocks and pocket watches, in-scale pipes, pipe cleaners and a leather tobacco pouch, a carpet bag, lap roll, favorite chair, a carpet and a completely trimmed in-scale German goose feather Christmas tree. Santa's contemporary-crafted sack is stuffed with hundreds of tiny antique toys. And an antique container is packed with an elaborate set of modern toy repair tools made by Jeffery. "All right! Now you've listed about half of what's there," the artists tease. "It's time to study the picture to find what you left out."

Kansas artist Barbara Kingman's Piney Woods Santa, designed in 1988, was inspired by the *Godey's Lady's Book* Christmas project published 120 years earlier! *Photograph courtesy of Barbara Kingman.*

In 1990, Barbara Kingman introduced a limited edition Sodbuster Santa Claus with arms and legs made of corncobs. "Sodbuster is a natural progression of the *Godey's* idea," the artist explained, "but he's more suited to the prairie states!" *Photograph courtesy of Barbara Kingman.*

From fine art to folk art and back again. Has any other theme in art history inspired such dizzyingly varied interpretations? Yet in studio after studio, artists gave the *same reason* for choosing Father Christmas as their creative focus. "My hope is that collectors won't just bring out my Santa doll for the December holidays. I want it displayed year round," we were told repeatedly. "That way, the Spirit of Christmas, with its power to *gentle* people, will go on and on, and the message conveyed through my artwork will do its bit to make the world a kinder place for us all."

A 13in (33cm) painted silk-over-composition Father Christmas made in 1980 by artist Paula Watkins. Paula crafted all the items in Santa's sack, including the puppet and fully-jointed teddy bear. *Photograph courtesy of Le Château Interiors.*

24in (61cm) tall. This droll fellow hopes to complete his annual whirlwind tour faster by using snowshoes! *Photograph courtesy of Mary Alice Byerly.*

Judy Grocki's basic cloth folk doll design has near infinite potential for variety. Pictured are Santas that average 6in (15cm) tall, each jointed at hips and shoulders and whiskered with sheep wool. From the left: Judy's Toy Santa, a Coca-Cola® Santa, a Victorian Santa with wizard's hood and a seated pink Santa with staff. *Photograph by Peter Groesbeck. Courtesy of Judy Grocki.*

Judy Grocki's Prairie Santa with Cow beside the artist's Working Santa Claus. *Photograph by Peter Groesbeck. Courtesy of Judy Grocki.*

Carved white pine Father Christmases by the McGrews. From left: Civil War Santa Claus, a menacing Black Peter, a tongue-in-cheek Southern Santa with a carved Confederate flag and a 10in (25cm) traditional Father Christmas. *Photograph by Peter Groesbeck. Courtesy of Johnny and Becky McGrew.*
RIGHT: The McGrews make this jointed Santa-with-Tree in two sizes. The one pictured is 40in (101cm) tall. His big brother is the author's height! Also shown is the McGrews' "roly" Santa. *Photograph by Peter Groesbeck. Courtesy of Johnny and Becky McGrew.*

An 8½in (22cm) *crocheted* Santa Claus by mini teddy bear artist Maggie Anderson. Different from Maggie's current tiny bears, this 1976 piece was special ordered by a private collector and is the artist's very first Santa doll! *Photograph by Peter Groesbeck. Courtesy of Linda Naccarato.*

The author's No. elf, a 12in (31cm) finger puppet assembled in Korea for American art toy designer Folkmanis® of Emeryville, California. *Photograph by Peter Groesbeck.*

The many objects that surround Frank and Jeffery's "most-travelled gentleman" include a fox terrier, an American flag and a hand-scribed list of good children. Of course, Frank and Jeffery's names are there! *Photograph courtesy of Le Château Interiors.*

Frank Hanley and Jeffery Guéno's magnificent Father Christmas vignette that began with a UFDC "giveaway" and an antique salesman sample trunk, then grew and grew... *Photograph courtesy of Le Château Interiors.*

Santa's "kit" includes hundreds of miniature antique and contemporary treasures. Frank and Jeffery continue to add to this extraordinary composition and admit they had no idea where the original idea would lead when they launched the project. *Photograph courtesy of Le Château Interiors.*

LEFT: In 1985, Oakland, California, artist Paul Pilgrim crafted this 16in (41cm) tall Father Christmas in the German candy container tradition. Head and shoulders lift off. Face, boots and hands are papier-mâché. Father Christmas wears a hand-quilted brown velvet robe trimmed with mink. The beard is rabbit fur. *Photograph courtesy of Paul Pilgrim.*

A 10in (25cm) jointed Santa peg doll by Richmond, Virginia, artist Fred Laughon. Santa's suit and cap, crafted by Helen and Nel Laughon, are red velvet trimmed with fluffy quilt batting. In the foreground stands a curious wooden toy. It could be a sheep or an odd hybrid chicken. Look again! It's RUDOLPH! *Photograph courtesy of Fred Laughon, Richmond, Virginia.*

Three tiny Santas to brighten holiday settings in any scale. Pictured are Janice Crawley's 1¾in (5cm) Canadian Santa Claus, a painted pewter Christmas gnome that certainly derives from an antique German mold and an extraordinary *tour de force* in miniature three-dimensional crocheting by upstate New York needle artist Dolores Szuba. *Photograph by Peter Groesbeck.*

Kim Bell

"We moved into our 100-year-old Victorian home in March 1984, and I quickly became a Victorian nut!" grins Virginian Kim Bell, whose robust, hearty Father Christmases reflect the period involvement that has become a way of life for this artist. Each holiday season since 1984, Kim has designed increasingly-elaborate decorations to fill her wonderful old house (there were *six* trees in 1990!). And in December of 1988, she made a first, "just-for-fun" Santa as a display focus for one of many elegant old-fashioned mantels. The initial idea was to build a figure around a commercially available head, but Kim could not find one that satisfied her. "So I bought a box of clay and made my own," she said.

Although she had never sculpted before and had no formal art background, Kim has always loved to work with her hands and enjoys testing her skill with varied media and techniques. Her first experimental Santas were rustic and dwarflike, very different from the exuberant pieces she creates today for an increasingly-enthusiastic collector following. And as she labored to master the technical intricacies and to refine the art and aesthetics of her Victorian Father Christmases, confidence in her ability to spread a very personal holiday message grew. Friends and family members, particularly husband Mike, encouraged her in her new work and, Kim is quick to add, without this encouragement, she would surely have given up early on. It was not an easy journey.

Today, Kim uses a flesh-colored clay that finishes like porcelain to sculpt her 24in to 27in (61cm to 69cm) one-of-a-kind Santas. "I use no molds," she told us. "I begin each piece with a ball of clay and develop it into what I imagine Father Christmas to look like, complete with wrinkles, smiling eyes and a whimsical yet realistic expression." Eyes are high quality glass; hair and beard are lamb's wool or goat hair. Boots are sculpted, then covered with suede; hands are carefully modelled to fit the mood and character of the individual piece. Father Christmas's body is a wire-and-wood armature fleshed out with cloth and stuffing.

The artist costumes each piece herself, using antique or antique-look fabrics and trimming. Santa's old-world costume usually includes a hooded coat in occasionally unexpected shades of soft burgundy, mauve, green and white, belted in leather and mink trimmed. Packs are real suede filled with period-type toys — brightly-painted wooden horses, handmade teddies, doll-scale books, toy horns and tiny dolls which she makes herself. Finished figures are signed, numbered and dated. Kim has full control of her compositions and makes purposeful, subtle use of her materials and accessories to drive home her message. Thus, a windblown Father Christmas with wild white hair and whiskers, frostbitten red cheeks and intense, riveting ice blue eyes echoes painted Father Frosts on Russian lacquerware boxes. A piece with warm eyes and a caring, tender expression wears a mink-edged cap that doubles as a dramatic halo and illuminates the Saint's benevolent face.

In addition to the traditional sacks of toys, many of Kim's Victorian Father Christmases carry evergreens or bundles of switches to punish bad boys and girls (in the old German tradition). Others clutch oak staffs or carry beautifully finished miniature sleds crafted from oak or walnut. Each figure is firmly mounted on an elegant wooden base.

All wooden accessories — oak staffs, tiny sleds, wooden stands — are crafted by Kim's talented husband, Mike Bell, who makes the turned hardwood bases from pieces of century-old flooring stripped from the attic of the Bells' Victorian home. "It seems right that a little bit of our actual house should become part of each figure," Kim reflected, "since the house itself had a lot to do with my becoming involved with Father Christmas in the first place!"

Apart from their beauty and link with the Victorian world she loves dearly, Kim tries to convey a very special message through her work. "A feeling I can't describe comes over me each December," she confided. I love the season and the gentleness it brings to the world. I beg collectors who purchase my Father Christmases not to put them away when the holiday ends. Keep them out. Keep them visible. Keep the Spirit and Magic of Christmas alive year round!"

William Bezek

"I have daily proof that the whole can exceed the sum of its parts!" grins California artist William Bezek, whose Santa sculptures have played a major role in their own designing since his first experimental project in November 1989. "When I completed my first Santa Claus, something took me by surprise," Will told us. "The figure had an extra quality, a wonderful personality that I certainly hadn't put there consciously. It seemed to have come to life by magic."

At 29, Will is a professional artist who was trained at The Academy of Art College in San Francisco. Key influences in his development are his mother's involvement with crafts and sewing, his father's woodworking interest and a deep love of Old Christmas, with its tradition of loving, caring and giving.

The artist was born in bustling, crowded Southern California and "discovered" Christmas at the age of 12 when his family moved to Washington State. He was thrilled by his first snowy winter, locked into a snowbound, small town atmosphere. Neighbors went caroling; children built snowmen in their front yards. Will and his family cut their own holiday tree. "It was like stepping inside a Currier and Ives print, a sentimental picture of what Christmas was supposed to be — a place where Father Christmas could be real."

Will first tried to recreate the complex emotions of those remembered winters through his Father Christmas sculptures three years ago, constructing his early figures much as he does his current, more elaborate pieces. "But those first Santas were made on a shoestring budget," he explained. "I used materials I found around the house — a white Halloween wig for hair (today I use lamb's wool) and antique upholstery fabric for costumes.

From the start, Will constructed bases for his Santas from turned hardwood moldings. Locating such moldings poses no problems for this artist whose nine to five professional track includes remodeling, interior design and carpentry. "If you put up dry wall for a living, architectural components like strip molding are easily come by," he joked.

Assembly methods for Will's 20in (51cm) Father Christmases are hardly conventional. He begins at the bottom, with a hollow base made from wide architectural molding. A heavy wire armature inside a cloth body is permanently mounted from inside the base. Boots or shoes are crafted and attached to the figure before mounting. The head is cast from the artist's original mold, using a rosin like clay overpainted with transparent washes to achieve the translucence of living flesh. "I paint the eyes rather than using glass eyes which look very static and blank to me," he confided, adding that "the eyes awaken a real personality in the face, and the shaping of wool eyebrows pushes the expression even further. I think carefully about this; nothing in my sculptures is done randomly. When I'm satisfied with the face, I attach the beard, then join the head and the body."

What follows is dictated by the figure's personality. "I work and they 'emerge.'" Will uses no definite patterns when costuming his Santas. Instead, he designs as he goes, creating period robes that combine recollections of Victorian prints and postcards with the colors and styling individual figures seem to demand. Whenever possible, he uses antique fabrics and trims, and if contemporary yardage must be incorporated into a costume, it is carefully antiqued and aged to suit the mood of the work of art. Santa's robes are trimmed with fake fur and imitation suede, since "real fur stripped from an animal for the sake of vanity doesn't fit with my concept of Father Christmas." Finally, Will stitches heavy wire into Santa's robes to facilitate shaping and sculpting of the flowing garments.

Once figures are dressed, they must be posed. This is a difficult task that requires concentration and a keen empathy with the subtle personality that has grown within each sculpture. Even accessories are chosen to complement the mood of individual figures. Some Santas are burdened with sacks stuffed with toys; others hold a single toy, like the old-style Father Christmas with rocking horse pictured here. Occasionally, Will's pieces carry only fruit or firewood. Note that the artist handcrafts some of the toys used with his Father Christmases. Others, purchased ready-made, are reworked — repainted, added to or aged — before taking their place in the bulging pack.

When a figure is complete, Will finishes the base. Wood is distressed, stained, antiqued and highlighted with rub-on gilt. Sometimes, the top of a base is covered with "snow." Antique finishing and gilding techniques are carefully chosen to complement the costume. Finally, Will varnishes the base and signs and dates the completed sculpture.

William Bezek admits that he is attached to these beautiful sculptures, each of which reflects his own artistic gift and schooling while maintaining an independent spirit and a personality uniquely its own. "I don't sell them right away," he admits. "I like to keep them around for awhile. Then I say goodbye and they go into the world to work their magic."

Beth Cameron

Beth Cameron's studio is a chalet-style building a short walk from her family's stone house in western Pennsylvania. The studio, nestled on a wooded bank adrift with springtime flowers and shaded by a century-old pine, provides the contained environment within which this extraordinarily talented and energetic artist works her special magic.

Inside, the rooms in which Beth crafts her Father Christmases are loaded with treasures, mystery and fun. "To costume and accessorize my work I collect everything — small-scale furniture, antique fabrics, trim and buttons, miniature books, leather, old fur coats — you name it and it's probably here someplace," Beth laughs, "waiting to be used for a child doll or Santa costume, to fill a pack or flesh out a vignette. Items I let pass me by I always end up regretting," she added. "I solved that one when I decided to let *nothing* pass me by!"

Thus, salesman sample chairs and rustic doll-size benches are suspended from nails and hooks hammered and screwed into walls and ceiling beams. Some chairs were found at flea markets and antique shops. Others are commissioned pieces, like the signed Windsors made for Beth by Richmond, Virginia based master craftsman Fred Laughon and by Gerald Headley of Williamsburg, Virginia. Drawers, cabinets and an attic storage area up a twisting staircase from the studio proper are all filled with the clutter of Beth's collections, thousands of old and new buttons, bits of veiling and Victorian handkerchiefs — endless objects, each electric with creative potential.

Family members and friends who contribute cast-off clothing and "findings" to the studio treasure trove are fascinated by Beth's power to "magic" old objects into exciting new ones. The artist, an ardent conservationist, has never consented to wear a fur coat or purchased a new pelt for studio work. Instead, the hair, moustaches and whiskers sported by her Santas, as well as the beaver, mink and raccoon trim on Victorian robes or American Santa jackets are cuttings from cast-off fur coats, flea market fox stoles, rabbit fur glove linings, snippets cut from Persian lamb coats, jackets and collars that date from the 1940s. "It's fun!" the artist explained. "You learn to look at things and see their potential for becoming other things. My Santas all have real fur, hair and beards, usually goat or lamb, but the source is *always* old fur."

An amusing story of old fur reused lies behind the bonny set of whiskers worn by a recent Beth Cameron Santa, for whom his own beard may well be the most bewildering object in his wide ranging experience. As a child, Beth told us, she wanted a dog desperately. Her parents did not share her longing, so in an unsuccessful effort at compromise one Christmas, they gave her a *toy* dog whose coat was genuine goat or sheep fur. Needless to say, that dog was not popular with Beth, and it soon moved to permanent quarters in a remote corner of the family attic. Beth's mother found it there a few years ago, a dismal survivor of dust, time and moths, and turned it over to the artist. The dog was welcome as a "second-rounder," since its real fur coat made ideal Santa whisker material. "So," Beth mused, "does that particular Santa Claus have dog whiskers? Or are they goat? Or lamb? It gets confusing sometimes!"

What is *not* confusing is that Beth Cameron is a supremely gifted artist whose creative output is straight from the heart, so much so, in fact, that years ago when the artist experienced a troubled time in her personal life, her Santas, elves and one-of-a-kind fantasy dolls echoed her inner distress, edging toward the grotesque creatures that populate Tolkienesque woodlands or live in the shadowy depths of a Brothers Grimm fairy forest. As the artist's troubles receded and her private world became more settled, the change was reflected in her studio art. It is almost possible to date Beth's work during the 1980s by the degree to which it echoes dark elves-of-the-hills elements or is a forthright statement of love within a cheerful, open and exquisitely detailed composition.

"From the beginning, I wanted to be an artist," Beth confessed, then described her happy student days at Carnegie-Mellon University, from which she graduated with honors and a degree in the fine arts. "It was while I was a student at Carnegie-Mellon that I saw a Christmas display at Kaufmann's Department Store in Pittsburgh — a wonderful jumble of dolls and ornaments imported from Europe. Among them was a German Father Christmas with a stockinette head. He cost $80 — the moon for a student in those days. I couldn't buy him, so I resolved to make my own."

In the course of the next three years, Beth quietly put aside fabric, trims and accessories to use for her Santa doll, then pulled everything out of the drawers where she had squirrelled it. "That first piece, with its funny cloth face, was a lark," Beth said, "and since he had been such fun, I went on to craft elves and more Santas."

For these, Beth turned her back on soft sculpture and used an imported sculpting clay, a medium she has grown to love. "From day one, I was fascinated by the waxy, translucent look of that material," she told us. "I liked the feel of it, to see how I could sculpt it, what fantastic creatures and marvelous faces I was capable of bringing to life with it." Some of these creatures were elves, drawn from memories of childhood readings, an example being the Swedish folk elf she crafted from recollections of the "tomte" who plays a definitive role in Marguerite de Angeli's classic, *Elin's Amerika.*

Beth attended her first New York Toy Fair in 1985, where she displayed one Santa Claus and a wide range of elves. She quickly realized that what was wanted was more Santas, and that her mid-1980s "elves with teeth" were overly realistic, even threatening to collectors. "It was fascinating to witness people's response to my art," Beth said, "and I was quick to shift to Santas and to make my figures less threatening."

Today, Beth's 14in to 22in (36cm to 56cm) Santas are among the most sought-after in the country, despite their four-figure price tags. "I have to charge a lot because of the investment in studio time that lies behind individually sculpted pieces. Also, there is a pretty steep monetary investment behind the figures — their antique accessories, the chairs, fabrics, beads, buttons, shawls and trimmings are all costly," she explained.

Each one-of-a-kind Beth Cameron Santa begins as a sculptured head and hands. "I think hands are as exciting as faces and just as filled with personality," she admits. Beth applies color to the clay directly, then fires the finished pieces. "I find the lines and wrinkles of age fascinating," she said. "They are character lines, the record of living. In fact, I'm intrigued by old faces, old hands, and it kills me sometimes to cover up a wonderful sculpted face with goat or lamb whiskers and a big moustache. I've left out the moustache a lot recently and left some Santas bald, just to avoid hiding the wrinkles.

It's funny, but collectors don't mind a bit. They know very well who the wonderful old gentleman is!"

When finished, Santa's head, hands and feet are attached to a body constructed from a positioned wire armature wrapped round with cloth (in the old crèche doll tradition) as well as with cotton batting, foam rubber — whatever gives the result the artist is striving for. Clothing is nonremovable and stitched to the figure, since the positioning of fabrics and accessories is an integral part of each artistic statement. For the same reason, recent Santas seated on chairs and surrounded by wide-eyed, wondering children have posed problems for Beth who wishes to retain full control of the positioning of components in her groups. "I want my pieces to stay where I've placed them," she said, "but I hate putting dolls into cases and cabinets, one sure way to fix everything permanently. Since I want everything out in the open and free looking, I've got a problem that won't be easy to resolve."

When Beth Cameron first began crafting Santas, she saw them as just that, whimsical figures and holiday gift bearers. Over time, her conception of this immortal gentleman has broadened and deepened, until today she tries to embody in each Santa Claus everything that is good, fine and joyous about Christmas as well as the visible signs of a long, well-lived life. Her Santas have become less a traditional symbol of the holiday and more a symbol of the beauty of age, with its power to draw children — in fact all humanity — into warm, meaningful, shared experience. "Love is up front with my Santas, not packages with ribbons and tinsel," the artist said with emotion."I'm moving toward more and more individualized faces," she added, "while at the same time the whole idea of Santa Claus is expanding to become a very personal statement of the universality of love and the beautiful interactions achieved by the young and old among us.

Lois Clarkson

"My Santas connect with the past," declares Lois Clarkson, whose extraordinary sculptures have a way of awakening memories of Christmases long gone. "European-born collectors who stop at my show table tell me wonderful stories out of their old-world heritage," she added, "because the figures I craft are the Christmas Men of their childhoods."

Understandably so, since most of Lois's joyous, intricately detailed Father Christmases derive from antique postcards in her vast collection and carry sacks or baskets brimming with real antique toys. Lois, who collected old toys and postcards long before she crafted her first Father Christmas in 1986, carefully matches the age and provenance of in-

scale toys and dolls with the Santas who tote them. Occasionally, a newly-acquired toy will inspire an entire sculpture. "For example, I found a World War II toy airplane, made of silk stretched over a wire frame, with a wooden propeller," she said. "The plane triggered an idea for my 3ft (1 meter) 1940s Santa. He holds the airplane in his hand and carries other toys of the same era in a bulging sack."

When Lois, a former elementary school teacher, crafted her first Father Christmas years ago, he had a papier-mâché head, painted eyes and a wire armature body wrapped around with papier-mâché and "fleshed out" with batting. "No more!" she laughed. "Papier-mâché was just too messy, so I switched to clay and loved it. I could push with my fingers and my Santa would start laughing. This is my medium; the potential is limitless."

Today, Lois Clarkson individually sculpts each Father Christmas head from a lump of clay, fits it with hand-blown German glass eyes and presses porcelain teeth into the clay jaw. Just as no two people are alike, so no two of her Santas are alike. She is proud, however, that with all their individual differences, each and every one of her Santa faces is anatomically correct. "I have studied sculpting books and have sculpted from life," she told us. "I also look in the mirror when I want to study how certain expressions affect the facial muscles. I've even been known to follow elderly gentlemen around to study their faces!"

Bodies and bases for this artist's sculptures are crafted by her husband, Jim, a carpenter/contractor who specializes in historic restoration. Jim carves each body form; Lois pads it with cotton batting, then dresses the completed figure in vintage fabrics and furs, old doll clothing, velvet coats, lengths cut from damaged antique quilts, old Amish children's shoes or in-scale wooden sabots.

The evocative power of her completed sculptures is clear from the stories related by collectors who see her work at shows. An older couple from The Netherlands ("themselves the epitome of Mr. and Mrs. Claus!") saw a Sinterklaas from Lois's studio, then told how each Saint Nicholas Eve (December 5th) the Dutch make great fun out of presents "from Sinterklaas." The ritual resembles a treasure hunt, and gifts fit the recipient's personality rather than impressing by their lavishness. Much of the fun is in the wrapping, which runs the gamut, from maddening stacks of nested boxes, each in paper and knotted with string, to naughty tricks like the ring gift the Dutch gentleman himself had received years earlier. "My ring was wrapped in layers and layers of bathroom tissue which had to be unwound very, very carefully, since I had no idea what was inside!"

On another occasion, a Hungarian show-goer described the differences between the European Father Christmas and the American Santa Claus. The European figure always has an alter ego, a dour personality (Black Peter, Belsnickle, and so forth) who metes out punishment for misdeeds. "In Hungary," the collector told Lois, "Father Christmas is called Mikulás and his companions, bad elves and devils called Krumpus, follow him out of the dark Austrian and Hungarian forests."

During the war years, life was hard and the gentleman could recall only one December during his childhood when Mikulás brought him a toy, a small wagon that fit in his hand. "When I was nine or ten, my faith in Mikulás began to waver," he explained "so my parents said there would be no Christ-

mas tree that year. I baby-sat the children next door on December 17th, and when I got home, I found a small tree on the table, decorated with shiny paper-covered candies, silvery sparklers and real candles. How had it gotten there? Had Mikulás left it? Or had the neighbors put it there while I was out? To this day, our old neighbors refuse to divulge the secret."

Of the many collector stories Lois has heard over the years, the most moving was told to her by a French woman who recognized one of the artist's dolls as the Père Noël of her own childhood. But when she peeked under the doll's cape, she was disappointed. There were no stars painted there. And she told Lois this story:

"I spent my childhood Christmases on my grandfather's farm outside Paris. He lived in an old farmhouse with a huge walk-in fireplace in the kitchen, and on Christmas Eve he would tell all the children to look up the huge chimney and watch for Père Noël. When we looked up and saw the night sky glittering with stars, my grandfather would say: "Look! There's Père Noël. I can see the stars under his cape!" Lois Clarkson has created many Père Noëls since that conversation, all with individually-sculpted faces, robed in various hues of antique velvet and with the traditional toy-filled French grape basket strapped to their backs but always, since meeting that French collector, the artist has remembered to paint stars inside Père Noël's cape.

Of the many Santas she has made over the years, the touch point with her *own* childhood memories is the American Coca-Cola® Santa Claus of the 1940s and 1950s. The day Lois crafted her first All-American Santa, she was startled by the complex emotional well she had tapped. And when she shopped for suitable vintage toys for her American Santa's sack, each called up long-forgotten associations from childhood.

"Santa Claus was a big part of our Christmas," she told us. "If my sister and I were arguing and a plane flew over our house, our mother would say: 'That's Santa and he's watching you!' We always waited for Christmas Eve to buy our family tree. It was bare and stuck in a bucket of water when we went up to bed, but the next morning it was decorated, illuminated and surrounded by colorful packages. I still can't figure out how 'Mr. and Mrs. Claus' did all that in one evening!

"The anticipation on Christmas morning was strained almost to the breaking point," Lois concluded with a grin, "since we children were required to wait in our room until Grandfather finished shaving — and he shaved the old-fashioned way, with a brush and a shaving mug. Then, at last, we went downstairs to a fantasy land come true — because Santa Claus had been there!"

Janice Crawley

There are Santa artists who work in wood or porcelain. Others prefer Fimo®, Sculpey® or Cernit®. Christmas craftspeople focus studio activity around old-world or new-world, traditional or "new wave" Father Christmases. Some make Santas exclusively; many divide the year between Santa art and other related craft interests. Manitoban Janice Crawley is the rare exception — at home in *any* medium, *any* scale and comfortable crafting anything!

Janice's work includes a 12in (31cm) white rabbit wearing a Queen of Hearts tabard and carrying a herald's trumpet and scroll, and a 6in (15cm) Tom kitten, miserable in the notorious blue suit of Miss Potter's *Tale...* The artist sews big classic teddies and crafts 1/144th-scale dolls for the dollhouse nursery. She works in materials that include muslin, plush and velvet, Fimo®, Sculpey®, wax-over-ceramic and porcelain. She has soft-sculptured large clowns and animals and crafted apple-headed street vendors with crab-apple-headed monkeys perched on their shoulders. Her tiny porcelain dishes for the dollhouse are snapped up by eager collectors from Western Canada to London, England. Her big cloth clowns, with their electric red hair and pseudomelancholic faces painted freehand with liquid embroidery colors, star in collections across Canada and the United States. We had never seen Santas crafted by this extraordinary lady. We asked her about this and she said: "Funny you mentioning that. I've wanted to make Santas for ages. I'll make them now!"

Janice Crawley has been involved with crafts of some sort for as long as she can remember. "Plasticine® (for modeling) was my favorite toy as a child," she explained during a recent visit. "My dolls were a close second; I still have all of them in a trunk in our basement. They are the wonderful composition dolls of the 1940s."

Janice would have preferred to study art after high school, but her family steered her toward a more practical profession, and she graduated from McGill University with a degree in Occupational Therapy in 1959. Even during those student years, she kept her hand in studio work. There were evening classes in oil painting and sculpture and, during a summer art course at Banff, she met her architect husband, Bryan, himself an artist and a master watercolorist. The couple settled in Winnipeg where Janice began her first serious experiments with clay. She purchased a kiln and started crafting slip-cast souvenir jugs and mugs. She hand built clay pots and funny animals for local craft shops and, while the Crawley's son, Devin, was young, she made stuffed toys and puppets for his nursery.

It was during those years that Janice discovered the Red River Exhibition Craft Fair, an exciting annual event in Manitoba. She was fascinated by the wide range of competitive categories at the fair and resolved to try her hand at each new craft technique that appeared on the Red River announcements. "The more categories they had, the more dolls I tried," she told us. "I used every imaginable medium — soft sculpture, plaster, glue and paint, ceramic heads dipped in beeswax and Fimo®-molded heads, hands and feet combined with soft bodies. One year, an Eskimo couple I did with Fimo® heads won 'Best in Show.' I was really proud since the competition is pretty keen."

This gifted artist had crafted dolls from porcelain for years before she discovered miniatures and made her first tentative experiments within dollhouse doll crafting. Oddly, her introduction to miniatures was through the kitchen door. "A friend collected small jugs and copper pots for a knickknack shelf, and I made a few jugs for her on my potter's wheel. I discovered a way to make tiny cups and teapots by cutting beads from my bead mold in half, then adding spouts, lids and handles. Next, I made a plaster mold from a toy tea set and started pouring and decorating tea sets of my own. The final step was to buy a commercial mold for dishes and to craft and market my own dollhouse-size dinnerware sets. I loved it!"

Once Janice discovered the miniature field that had taken Eastern Canada by storm in the early 1980s, she expanded her porcelain offerings, then tried her hand at teenie tiny porcelain dolls for the dollhouse. They were an instant success.

Those first "tinies" were developed from molds designed from small plastic toys belonging to herself and to a Winnipeg friend. "After I poured the dolls," she said, "I had trouble removing them from the molds without breakage, so I cut the arms at the shoulders and the legs at the hips, poked tiny holes in the limbs and bodies with a needle and strung the parts together with beading wire. The entire process worked beautifully, and the finished dolls retained the delightful detail of the plastic originals. I had trouble cleaning their small arms and hands at first and a number of 'tinies' broke, but my fingers soon became sensitized to the scale I was working in."

True to form, once Janice decided to "make those Santas," she plunged into experiments with varied materials and scales and was soon completely caught up in her new project. In fact, July of 1990 will probably go down in history as Santa Claus month in the Crawley's basement studio. "I am up to my ears in furry pieces!" Janice wrote to us from Winnipeg.

When, weeks later, we saw the results of Janice's Santa Claus party, we were dazzled by the artist's virtuosity. She had crafted a high-fashion soft toy pig Santa 10in (25cm) tall, sporting a huge brown velvet sack crammed with toys and candy. A 6½in (19cm) jointed fur fabric seated teddy bear with a shy smile wore a charming red velvet jacket and cap trimmed in fluffy white. One of the artist's favorite storybook characters, Tom Kitten, took another bow, miserable as ever in *clothes*, this time a cumbersome Father Christmas outfit. A dollhouse scale "Ho-Ho-Ho" Santa Claus, a Coca-Cola® poster look-alike, stood tall and joyous at 6in (15cm), and what may well be the world's smallest Santa posed in diminutive splendor atop a shiny Canadian brass thimble!

Janice's month-long Santa Claus party also produced a tiny porcelain Santa pig and cat and a large "antique" wax-over-wood Father Christmas with a decidedly European flavor, dressed in a brown, fur-trimmed cap and a long coat with a rope sash. This figure holds the symbolic evergreen as well as a leather sack and basket stuffed with old-fashioned, in-scale toys and dolls, many crafted by the artist herself.

Tiny, huge, vintage and modern, human, pig, cat and teddy, cloth, wax-over-wood and porcelain — this extraordinary artist moves effortlessly from medium to medium, from scale to scale. Each piece she makes is unique. Each piece is exquisitely thought through and executed. And, as collectors know and readily agree, each and every work of art created by Canada's Janice Crawley reflects the joy and spirit of fun that characterize this very special artist.

Glenda Fletcher

There are porcelain Santas, Fimo®, Cernit®, papier-mâché Santas, carved wood Santas and Santas with shoulderplate heads and wire armature bodies wrapped around with cloth in the manner of 18th-century Italian crèche figures. They are, one and all, adult collector pieces and, while many are gorgeous, three-dimensional portrayals of the Spirit of the Season, they are, in the end, meant only to be looked at. They are not huggable.

Not so the "down home" rag doll Santas crafted by Glenda Fletcher of Litchfield, Maine. "To me, Santa is sharing — sharing the joy, hope and good will that the holiday brings," Glenda told us. "I make Santas in the hope that they will keep the Christmas spirit alive throughout the year. To see one of my dolls tucked into the fold of the arm is the reward of my work, assurance that he is appreciated, recognized as a friend and a visible symbol of the holiday and all that it represents."

Glenda Fletcher is a brilliant craftsperson of the old school, in all the best ways 100 percent State of Maine! She grew up in a tightly-knit Maine farm family where there was an abundance of love, but little money to spare for frills like fancy toys. So she and her two sisters made their own, especially cloth dolls. Those childhood projects provided fundamental doll-crafting knowledge the artist continues to draw on today.

"We learned to sew at home, of course," Glenda said, "but the *real* lessons were through a wonderful 4-H teacher who taught us to be proud of our work and to be satisfied with nothing short of perfection. She was very patient with our mistakes, and I remember well removing stitches, turning fabric from side to side to unravel the seams — and always with an eye to please our teacher and to win those coveted blue ribbons in 4-H competitions."

Over the years, sewing became the chosen medium of expression for this talented artist who explained that "it gives me an opportunity to create, and if I'm not creating something, I have an empty feeling inside me." So when this lady, who has been sewing and "into crafts" as far back as she can remember, decided to specialize in Santa dolls in 1987, it hardly surprised friends and family that Glenda chose cloth dolls as her focus. What *did* surprise everyone, however, was the wizardry she brought to cloth and the highly individual and amazingly lifelike posable, lovable Santas that quickly filled her comfortable Maine kitchen.

Glenda uses no pattern for her one-of-a-kind Santas which average 18in to 24in (46cm to 61cm) tall ("Smaller than that just doesn't seem like a doll to me!"). The doll body is muslin, selected because it is a comfortable fabric to work with and feels like living flesh. Muslin, the artist asserts, is soft and warm to the touch, feels like skin and gives Santa a cuddly warmth. Figures are jointed at shoulders, elbows, hips and knees and have cloth or wooden hands and feet. If of wood, they are hand-whittled by neighbor Wally Trott whose work, Glenda believes, gets better and better.

Faces for Glenda's dolls are sculpted cloth formed according to her own unique craft recipe which, like most aspects of her art, differs from techniques used by fellow Santa artists at work in the country today. Every Santa face starts as a square of cotton muslin immersed in a sizing mixture, then placed over a basic form. When the face begins to set, the artist hand models individual facial detail. After the piece has thoroughly dried, she paints it, applying the pigment with a small brush, her fingers, even with the flat of her hand. Hair, moustaches, eyebrows and whiskers are natural fiber, either pure mohair or Icelandic sheep's wool. Recently, Glenda has begun to purchase lamb's wool on the hide, then cutting, positioning and applying it to her Santa heads with a hot glue gun. If cotton muslin faces retain wrinkles after molding and painting, the artist leaves them there, in the belief that, along with purposefully built-in wrinkles, the extra ones add character and individuality to the face.

"From the start, my biggest challenge was to make the face as lifelike as possible," Glenda said, adding, "I wanted the face to glow like a winter fireplace. Keeping the features intact and getting a softer skin tone on the cloth is very important to me. If my Santas don't look back at the person smiling at them, they're not my dolls at all. They're just handfuls of stuffing and cloth."

Dressing the dolls is a "fun thing," Glenda declares, since the colors and cut of Santa's suit are invariably dictated by the expression and overall mood of his freshly painted features. The artist uses only vintage furs and homespun fabrics for each "down home" Santa Claus suit. "I dress every Santa in the time frame in which I've spent my own life," she added, "mostly because I have a hard time imagining him any other way. I try to think of his face as a father or a brother, an uncle or a neighbor, then dress him accordingly."

Glenda Fletcher's warm-hearted Santas relax in wooden rockers, doll-size chairs slipcovered in tiny print fabric or upholstered in real leather. They sit in sleighs or at kitchen tables "enjoying donuts and coffee," or they hold hammer and saw and stand beside the proverbial workbench. They come barefoot, booted or slippered. They pose in specially designed Maine buckboards, sit beneath Christmas trees, ride traditional rocking horses and daydream beside astonishing sky-rocking horses.

"Every single accessory," the artist told us proudly, "is handcrafted right here in the state of Maine, then painted and finished as a one-of-a-kind piece." Glenda's talented sister, Sandra Robinson, makes all the leather boots, shoes and slippers worn by cloth-footed Santas. Rocking chairs and other art furniture accessories are signed craft masterpieces by Sharon Tilton. Specialty woodwork is by Paul Chizmas and Arthur Allen, and Wally Trott combines unusual talent and a whimsical sense of humor to hand whittle his very special Santa feet and hands as well as cherry or rosewood pipes so that, in our imaginations at least, the "smoke can encircle each head like a wreath!" — a respectful bow to Clement Moore!

"I love what I do and keep coming up with new ideas for accessories, props and improvements for my work," Glenda said. "Each and every doll is 'homespun' in my kitchen as a reminder that the home and family are what make the *real* joy of the holiday season. Every Santa is signed, but I don't number them. How can you put a number on Santa Claus!" And since each of Glenda's charming dolls is a one-of-a-kind handcrafted figure, no piece exactly duplicates any other. The only thing all Santas made in Glenda's kitchen assuredly share is love!

Judy Fresk

"I call my dolls 'Gift Givers,' not 'Santas,'" Connecticut artist Judy Fresk told the author, adding "It's *costuming* the dolls that I find fascinating — designing and sewing outfits that echo different cultures and periods out of history. Every culture has a traditional gift giver figure," she added, "but not all of them are Saint Nick."

As a child, Judy was fascinated by textiles and costumes and devoted endless hours to the designing and sewing of clothing for her many dolls. Later, she studied costume and textile history at the University of Connecticut where she earned a degree in Fashion Design. In 1980, the artist combined her many interests and became a doll maker. It was an ideal career choice that focused Judy's training and love of design, painting, wig making, pattern making and the adventures of searching for and working with exquisite fabrics.

"It was meeting and spending time with a wonderful lady, Elizabeth Fisher, that set me thinking about a doll-making career," Judy confessed. "Mrs. Fisher was an inspiring teacher, a fantastic personality who overcame physical handicaps to share knowledge and experience gleaned across nearly 90 years. She really *believed* in miniatures, dolls and in the importance of keeping old doll-making and hand-craft techniques like lace-making and tatting alive."

Readers may know that Elizabeth Fisher was the *modus operandi* behind the classic *Doll Trader* journal. She also authored a number of books that are increasingly collectable today. Among these are two, each designed to look like a hand-written manuscript, and titled *Doll Stuff Notebook* and *Miniature Stuff Notebook*. The first is literally stuffed with detailed notes about doll repair, collecting, crafting, painting, wigging; the second describes innumerable ingenious ways to craft miniature dollhouse furnishings from ordinary objects around the home. Both books are typical of their author, for whom "sharing" was what life was all about.

"Elizabeth Fisher was a tremendous influence in the development of many doll makers, including myself," Judy Fresk told us. "She taught me to sculpt a head, to mold, to tat. And she taught me to appreciate the special magic of the doll artist's world." That magic electrified the atmosphere of the astonishing Connecticut home in which Mrs. Fisher hostessed evening meetings for doll and handcraft enthusiasts, meetings that often lasted into the wee hours. Elizabeth Fisher's home reflected her extraordinary, eccentric personality. "The interior was a maze of little paths between metal shelving loaded with boxes and paper bags, all unlabeled and filled with the bits and pieces of her collections. Mrs. Fisher knew without checking exactly where everything could be found. To give you an idea of the state of that house," Judy grinned, "I can tell you that it was impossible to walk around the table where group meetings were held. There was clutter everywhere! The room was small; the shelves were close together. So you had to leave the table and loop your way through two other rooms, then double back across the first room to gain a position on the side of the table opposite the point where you started!"

More than a decade has passed since her exciting, unconventional introduction to the doll maker's art. Today, Judy Fresk makes 16 different Gift Givers, each an edition limited to 1500 and sought by serious collectors across the United States and Canada. These figures are 18in (46cm) tall with porcelain head, hands and feet. Porcelain components for every piece are cast from identical molds. Hand finishing — painted features, sanding, wigging and most particularly costuming — help individualize the figures. Doll bodies are stuffed muslin; beards and hair are plaited wool crepe or mohair imported from England. The costumes worn by these limited edition dolls are all designed from contemporary fabrics, trims and accessories, and Judy relishes the challenge of locating modern materials with a vintage look. Because materials are new, the artist's production costs are comparatively low, and she gladly passes this advantage along to collectors.

For the past few years, Judy has also made costly, one-of-a-kind Gift Givers very different from her more reasonably priced limited edition pieces. Each one-of-a-kind figure measures 26in (66cm) tall, with porcelain head, hands, boots and a soft body. Hair and whiskers are luxuriant Tibetan goat fur. "These pieces are important art experiences for me," Judy said. "Each is developed as a composition that integrates antique fabrics, color, extraordinary old-time needlework detail and visually pleasing design. As a matter of fact, I see them as studies in design *first* and Gift Givers second."

Bringing a one-of-a-kind Gift Giver to life starts with the discovery of an extraordinary piece of antique clothing, generally an exquisitely detailed Edwardian blouse perfectly sized by an accommodating seamstress a century ago to be cut up and reworked as a Judy Fresk doll costume.

"I unearth antique clothing for my figures in the most wonderful places," the artist told us. "I search through piles of old garments at antique shows, rummage in bins in antique shops and haunt vintage clothing shows. What I search for is detail in old handwork that adapts well as cuffs, puffed sleeves, shirring and tucks for my Gift Givers. I also watch for wonderful old beaded and embroidered handbags, change purses and sachet bags that convert to magnificent toy sacks." A case in point is one Gift Giver pictured here, whose sack began life as a sachet bag covered with fine hand-embroidered detail stitched onto a white leather ground. When antique dealers first learned that Judy cut up and reworked their priceless vintage treasures, they were mortified. But when the artist showed them slides of her finished dolls, the dealers were won over, many so completely that they now seek out likely antique garments for her and telephone about things they feel she may be able to use.

Each time something rare and old that is useful does in fact turn up, Judy spots its potential right away. "I can look at a finely detailed hundred-year-old garment and rework it in my mind as a doll costume," she said, adding, "Before I even buy the garment, I visualize how I'll integrate it in the construction of my piece. I may change my mind about details as I develop the composition, but the *basic idea* is formed by the time that piece of fabric comes into my workroom."

Lynn Haney

"I have always 'made things;' as a child I loved to cut up paper, fabric, cardboard, wood, anything I could get my hands on," declares Lubbock, Texas, artist Lynn Haney. "With glue, straight pins, nails, tacks, needle and thread, I created assemblages, using as many different materials and techniques as possible. I still do that," Lynn adds. "Doll making is, after all, the ultimate rich combination of assorted media."

Lynn Haney was raised in a small Texas town that lacked theater, museums and large libraries. As a result, he turned inward, feeding his active imagination on traditional fairy tales and loving the drawings of faces and costumes that brought the stories to life. In college, he majored in Art Education where required courses included jewelry making, print making, pottery, weaving, metal sculpture and more. That broad-based education in studio art has been put to excellent use in his doll-making workshop but, before he became a full-time doll artist, Lynn taught in Texas public schools and free-lanced during summers and holidays. "After six years of this rigorous routine," Lynn told us, "I realized that although I loved teaching, the classroom was holding me back. So I left the schools and entered the business world. I had a sales position for four years before my doll making developed into a full-blown business in its own right. Our first solo flight year was 1986 and we haven't turned back for a minute since then."

Today, Lynn's studio creates wizards and peddler dolls in addition to Father Christmases and Santas which are the artist's first loves. In the Haney household, where Christmas has always been the favorite season, Lynn made his first Christmas dolls as heirlooms-of-the-future for his twin daughters. When he realized that nostalgia, art and sentiment are part of the universal Christmas spirit, however, Lynn began designing holiday dolls for today's Christmas collectors, in hope that they will pass them on to the potential Christmas collectors among their descendants.

Lynn Haney Christmas dolls are available as limited editions or as one-of-a-kind pieces crafted from start to finish by the artist himself. For each limited edition, Lynn sculpts head and hands for the prototype, then makes a mold in which components are cast in wood composition "which provides a particularly nice surface for painting." Lynn constructs the wire armature, cloth-stuffed body and costumes the prototype himself, before assigning production duties to the seven highly-trained craftspeople who staff his Texas studio. "Finished limited edition dolls range from 18in to 48in (46cm to 122cm) tall and are dressed in a variety of fabrics," the artist said. "For these production pieces, we use velvets, wools and blends. My one-of-a-kind Father Christmases, with faces and hands sculpted in low-fire clay, are dressed in vintage wools and antique fabrics and trims. I particularly enjoy the many different interactions within the studio — supervising production of limited editions that derive from my prototypes and creative experiments in one-of-a-kind doll making. And occasionally, the patterns come together when the idea that sparked a one-of-a-kind Santa is reinterpreted as a limited edition piece."

Father Christmas artist Lynn Haney calls himself a lucky fellow. He works a busy 60 to 80 hour week doing something he never tires of. "In today's automated, computerized world, I am creating with my hands for a public that responds to top quality hand-crafted work and is willing to support artists who make it. My biggest enemy is TIME," Lynn grins. "I want to create more and more and explore new avenues in doll making. It takes all the self-discipline I can muster to stay on course and maintain the level of studio production!"

Lew and Barbara Kummerow

Lew and Barbara Kummerow, whose reproduction vintage toys and fantasy artifacts are virtually indistinguishable from their antique prototypes, have lived under the spell of antique toys for as long as they can remember. Their California home is filled with treasures culled from the nursery cupboards of the past; their library shelves are packed with books about old playthings, Christmas-related objects and toy history; their studio is a magic room where long-dead crafts once again become living art.

Since childhood, Lew Kummerow's empathy for things Victorian has gone hand in hand with exceptional artistic gifts and a fascination with the way craft work was designed and assembled in 19th century cottage industry days. As a small boy in Chicago, he spent his allowance on old-fashioned toy soldiers from Marshall Field & Co. By the time he reached his teens, the collecting passion and hands-on interests fused, and Lew began purchasing unpainted military miniatures which he finished himself, then enhanced with delicate applied detail.

Lew met his wife, Barbara, in college, where he majored in industrial art and she studied the studio arts. After marriage, Lew taught drafting and architecture in high school and, during weekends and vacations, he and Barbara scoured antique show booths, auction rooms and dusty shops in search of (in those days affordable!) antique toys. The day came when, as a "fun experiment," the Kummerows tried to replicate several toys they knew from books, as well as favorite examples from their expanding personal collection. To increase the challenge, they limited themselves to techniques and materials available to the original craftsmen. But what started as a hobby-related game, quickly evolved into serious preoccupation with surprisingly sophisticated art from the past. The proportion of time given over to solving technical and research problems related to these studio projects kept increasing until, by the mid 1970s, the Kummerows realized the time had come to transform their hobby into a full-time business. Today, the couple's 1in (3cm) = 12in (31cm) dollhouse scale replicas of toyland Victoriana have a place in most of the country's important miniature collections, and Lew's magnificent, exact size replicas of antique Santa art are prized by Christmas collectors across the country.

"Our own collection includes German and Japanese Santas that date from the 1880s to 1930," Barbara explained. "Now that antique examples have become so expensive, Lew is making reproductions in very limited editions and in the exact size of the originals. Our hope is that our replicas (or new issues!) of old toys, tree ornaments and candy container treasures will give the same pleasure to other collectors that the originals have given to us."

There are no jarring notes or anachronistic details on an antique Santa "reissue" from Lew Kummerow's studio. Each copy is made directly from the original, which means that dimensions, details, colors, textures, even the weight and "feel" of the piece are completely true to the prototype. Materials used, as with the couple's early experiments in the 1970s, remain as true to the original piece as possible. "Our Santa figures are made from a plaster-like material; the old German Santas were molded plaster with some kind of fiber filler," Barbara said. "Arms and legs are wire or elastic, beards are rabbit fur, heads, hands and boots are molded directly from the antique figures and painted as exact copies. Chips, cracks and stains present on the originals appear on our repros as well. Clothing patterns are also taken directly from the originals, then made up in 'antiqued' cloth — flannel or felt usually. Lew arranges the garments so that the creases, folds and overall timeworn appearance are precise copies of the piece he is copying from. In fact, when we sent a group of Lew's Santas to be photographed for the *Santa Dolls* book, we included one antique piece among them since the repro wasn't finished yet,"

Barbara added with a mischievous smile. "Neither the author nor the photographer could guess which piece was the old one. We had to tell them!"

Occasionally, as with the rare Althof-Bergmann Santa-in-Sleigh with goats bell toy from the 1880s pictured on page 109, Lew had no antique collectible to work from in the studio. In fact, there are only two or three known examples of this magnificent, fragile treasure in existence, one of which recently sold at auction for $75,000. Recreating the Althof-Bergmann piece from an art book photograph was a rare challenge that Lew thoroughly enjoyed. Working only from the two-dimensional illustration and a knowledge of the overall dimensions of the antique toy which were noted in the photo caption, Lew developed his own molds, then cast components in materials nearly identical to the prototype and finished his one-of-a-kind repro of this rarest of rare toys so that it echoes the intricacy and patina of the Victorian original. The sleigh is formed sheet metal; goats are tin. Santa has a plaster face, crepe paper costume and wears white cotton gloves. Like the antique prototype, Lew Kummerow's repro bell toy measures an impressive 9in by 18in (23cm by 46cm).

Lew Kummerow has become so attuned to the spirit of antique Santa art over the years and so adept at reproducing it for today's collectors that it seemed only natural to him to take the final step, cross the time line and create *new* art in the mood of the old. An example of the artist's "original" antique Santa candy containers is the 7in (18cm) tall impish Santa-in-tree-trunk pictured here. The piece is faithful to the design, mood and style of its century-old ancestors and is living proof that occasionally an artist manages to achieve the impossible, to merge with the past and create within the pure tradition of a bygone age, untinged by the culture of his own times!

Deborah Lange-Henderson

"For me, the big moment came in my thirties, the day I discovered doll collecting and that there were crowds of people like me — that I didn't really have to grow up and pretend dolls were only for children. That day," says Missouri artist Debbie Henderson, "a whole new world opened." It was a world that linked the intense inner experience of an imaginative childhood with the evolving skill of a future artist, whose stunning talent gives form and substance to a unique inner vision.

Debbie's early years were filled with love, family, storybooks and dolls ("by the time I was thirteen, I had at least forty and I loved every one!"). White Chicago Christmases meant festive gatherings of relatives, celebration, Christmas trees, the smell of greenery, the sound of laughter, toys, dolls

and exciting new books. "My German grandfather and my mother had little Christmas joy when they were growing up," Debbie confided. "Our Chicago holidays were the Christmases they had missed, and they spoiled us all with love, family and toys."

Books, especially romances and the fantastic, were Debbie's world throughout childhood, though she could not have foreseen how she would eventually reshape the myriad images those early stories impressed on her brain. Illustrations were as important as texts, she told us, adding, "Oh, those illustrations! I spent many hours just looking and looking at them. And when television moved into our house in the early '50s, another powerful visual world opened. Puppets, magical frogs, clowns — what more could a child ask for?"

From the witches, dwarfs, giants and creatures of the woods that populate childhood storybooks, Debbie graduated to romantic movies, with swashbuckling heroes, lavish sets, castles, dungeons, the rolling seas and misty forests. "There was Errol Flynn, Doug Fairbanks, Tyrone Power! Pirates, the French Court, Queen Elizabeth and Sir Walter Raleigh — all the romance of those lost centuries. Costuming in those movies — WOW! Stage sets — WOW! Detail — WOW! I could go on forever," she reminisced. "There was detail, detail, detail. My eyes missed nothing, yet I was oblivious to the impact it would have on my own art in later years."

Ironically, this gifted lady's art grades through high school were only middling. ("I was frustrated by all the things my *mind* could see but couldn't translate into images.") After high school, Debbie turned her back on the arts and entered the business world. She married her talented cabinetmaker husband, Mark, and their daughter, Cati, was born on Valentine's Day. Theirs was a familiar, comfortable lifestyle, except, Debbie laughs, "about twice every year I would be driven by something inside me, and out would come pencils, chalk and paper. I put house and family aside to spend my time at the drawing board, until whatever it was was out of my system!"

Everything changed in her early thirties when illness forced Debbie to retire from business and rethink the future. She read; she cooked; she self-taught herself sewing by running up 21 Barbie® doll dresses as a Christmas surprise for Cati. And she used her new sewing skills and innate love of fine materials and design to craft a rag doll from a pattern discovered at the public library. The rag doll project was such fun, she made more, then took them to a local craft show to see what would happen. The dolls were a success, but it was the discovery of the doll collecting world that made the day memorable. That was a revelation for Debbie, who had long believed the child's world of romance, fantasy and dreams was closed to her forever.

"The next step — boy, was I excited! — was the local craft store. Clay! I had always wanted to work with clay but knew nothing about it. I purchased one of every type on the shelf. Most proved difficult to work with, not giving me what I wanted, although I wasn't quite sure what it was I did want. I found one that was interesting, clean, easy to work with, but it was much too heavy If I was going to do faces and attach them to bodies. I called the manufacturer and found he had another, lighter clay. He sent it to me, and the rest, I guess you'd say, was history."

Debbie "played" with her clay, "doing faces — pretty faces, strange faces, wondering all the time where they were coming from." Experiments led to wood-and-wire bodies with jester heads and costumes and a major display at the local (Kansas City) Renaissance Festival. Two months later, she had her first one-woman gallery show ("with the proprietor telling everyone I was in my embryonic stage!") Perhaps the most interesting thing about those early, problem-solving days grew out of Debbie's lack of formal schooling in studio arts. "If you don't know it can't be done, you just figure out a way to do it," she grinned, adding, "One of my most enlightening experiences was to find out you don't have to do things the way other people do in order to be right or good; that just maybe you know something they don't and it just might be better. It was a revelation, a liberation!"

By the time Debbie Henderson had her second gallery show, she was looking for ways to turn her hobby into a livelihood. Then followed several years of marketing efforts, agent contacts and increasing magazine coverage of her unusual and exciting approach to doll and, particularly, to Santa sculpting. A big question from the start was whether to focus on quantity or quality. "Quality won, of course," Debbie said. "But it was a gamble. We knew it would take time for people to understand and be willing to accept what we were doing. But by our third year, business had tripled, and our followers knew that if they saw gold beads, they were 14K; if fur, it was real. Materials and trims were antique or European, the best we could find." Even when volume of sales forced Debbie to add molded limited editions to her one-of-a-kind originals, she refused to compromise quality. "We found a superb mold maker and a chemist. Our molding material is unlike anything else available on the world market. The only way *we* can tell the prototype originals from molded heads and hands is by touching them. To the eye, they are indistinguishable."

Debbie still does all the designing for her figures, which are marketed under the name "Drollerics®". She personally paints and beards her Santas, while wooden bases and many wood accessories are crafted by her cabinetmaker husband and partner, Mark Henderson. Other accessories — carved reindeer (by Kansas artist Brad Nicholas), stuffed teddies and other stuffed animals for Santa's pack (by Trudy Jacobson), specially-commissioned woven cloths, bent willow chairs — all are from the workshops of first-rate craftspeople Debbie has located in a never-ending search for the best components to complement her Santas, Nicholases, Nikkis and flower faeries. "Potters, basket makers, weavers and spinners all work with us," Debbie explained. "And of course there is my right hand, my keeper Jimmie Bateman. God sent her to me in 1989; she is a nationally-known miniatures artist who fell in love with my 'babies' and now works in our studio daily."

Where that studio stops and the Hendersons' home starts is the $64 question! The family lives in a rambling Kansas City house built in 1912. Debbie's *official* studio, gorgeously fitted out by husband Mark with custom built-in cupboards, shelves and cutting tables, includes an old sleeping porch with windows on three sides. "It's a high, airy dream place surrounded by trees," the artist smiled. "I feel as though I live in a tree house, watched by squirrels, woodpeckers and robins as I work."

For this artist, for whom the fantasy, romance and doll world of an imaginative childhood are tightly interwoven with studio life in Kansas City today, it is not surprising that Santa art claims an ever greater fraction of floor and shelf space. By 1991, the studio had overtaken the entire house. Faery dolls now occupy an over-sized nonfunctional fireplace. Peddlers and wood elves as well as a 6ft (nearly 2m!) Santa dominate living room and hall. "I just dismantled my 4ft (122cm) wood wizard who used to reside in our living room," Debbie laughed. "The closets are filling up with things other than clothing. The original bathroom has been converted to fabric storage. The garage is no longer, and we're wondering what next! Mark and I love this huge old house, but it's truly a Santa and fantasy place to reside. There's no getting away from it!"

Jocelyn Mostrom

To look at Jocelyn Mostrom's elegant, ethereal child dolls, angels and Father Christmases, it is hard to believe that each began life inside a bale of Mexican cornhusks wrapped round with steel bands. "But it's true," explained the artist, who is nationally known for her sophisticated work with a material many still associate with quaint and primitive folk art. "Those bales measure about 3ft by 3ft (1m by 1m) and are incredibly heavy," Jocelyn continued. "I cut the bands and thousands of rough, unruly husks explode all over the floor. It takes months, working with friends, to sort them, process them and dye them in preparation for my doll making."

Historically, cornhusk dolls were a by-product of pioneer farming in cultures where goods were scarce and nothing was wasted. When the corn harvest had been reduced to soup, bread, pudding, corn mash whiskey, corncob pipes and johnny cake, the husks were stuffed into mattresses or made into dolls and toys. In *American Folk Dolls* (New York, Alfred A. Knopf, 1982), author Wendy Lavitt writes that few of the old cornhusk dolls were saved by their owners. "They were simply swept into the dustbin or destroyed in play. Small animals found their sweet kernels tasty and little children easily tore them apart." (p. 35)

The few antique cornhusk treasures that *have* survived into our own time are museum pieces today. Each was lovingly home crafted from husks that were first soaked in water to make them soft and pliable, then rolled and wrapped to create dolls which were painted with natural dyes — berry or vegetable juices, earths, crushed leaves, tree bark. Hair was corn silk; hats were dried sunflowers trimmed with chicken feathers; clothing was scraps and snippets from the rag bag. Cornhusk doll making was revived as a marketable American folk craft during the difficult WPA days of the 1930s, and several examples of delightful wrapped, rolled and braided cornhusk dolls appear in *The Index of American Design*.

Jocelyn Mostrom has an encyclopedic knowledge of cornhusk doll history. At the same time, her own studio work with this folk medium represents an innovative (and exciting!) departure from traditional patterns.

"I grew up on a farm in Maine," the artist told us, "where my New England father taught us to be resourceful, and my mother, who shares my lifelong love of dolls and the arts, inspired me to make and dress dolls in all imaginable materials. She taught me that whatever the dream, there was a way to succeed with it." That encouragement and support pushed Jocelyn to try her hand at all kinds of crafts over the years. She sewed, created millinery confections, gardened, became expert in drying and preserving flowers, worked in wood, papier-mâché and cornhusk, collected fabrics, trims, tiny jewels, metal findings and bits of antique lace. At the same time, she pursued studies at Colby College and Harvard's School of Education, taught school for eight years, tried her hand at dress designing and raised her own family.

During her dressmaking years, Jocelyn was commissioned to dress a group of antique dolls. Since she was "playing" with cornhusk at the time, she designed 19th century fashions in miniature and used cornhusk in lieu of fabric. The experiment was tremendously successful. "I would *never* go back to fabrics," she states emphatically. "Husks are much more exciting. Each one has its own unique characteristics. Some are rippled from pressing against the kernels underneath. Throughout soaking and dyeing, they never lose their ripple patterns and make up beautifully as doll skirts. Very smooth, thin husks are ideal for faces and skin. And sometimes the dyeing process brings surprises — wonderful moiré effects that make gorgeous fabrics. Some people mistakenly believe that the 'husks' are the thick outer leaves of the corn. They aren't. Cornhusk art uses the very thin inner leaves that lie just above the silk."

Jocelyn's dolls have posable, wire-armature bodies, and figures are positioned to give the impression of living motion. Once a wire frame is complete, the artist adds a porcelain or cornhusk head and hands, then fills out the body with cornhusk. Costumes are made from carefully-dyed husks and finished with trims, laces, jewels and filigrees from Jocelyn's vast collection. Wigs are mohair, lamb's wool, human hair, goat hair or flax.

Most dolls from this Maryland studio have porcelain faces, all of which are hand-painted in soft tones by the artist. For one-of-a-kind or very limited edition dolls and Santas, she hand sculpts, molds, presses and paints cornhusk faces, a task that may require up to 60 hours per doll. Designs for new dolls draw on the artist's vast experience with fabrics and fashion history. "All these designs are already in my head," she smiled. "It's just a question of running after them and capturing them! I enjoy that part of my doll work most of all and set aside special time after the busy holiday season to do nothing but work on new design ideas."

Jocelyn loves her child dolls with their Kate Greenaway pinafores, Christopher Robin suits and exquisite *bébé* Jumeau costumes. "But the most fun to costume are the angels and the Santas," she confided. "There are so many traditions, so many different cultural backgrounds for Father Christmas. Every one of them provides a world of creative opportunity in doll and doll costume design. I love it!"

For this artist, who loves what she does and does it exquisitely, no line of demarcation separates work from play. "I'm doing wonderful things and having a wonderful time," she said. "I only wish that every human being could be blessed with an equally great area in which to play. I learn all the time; I have the opportunity to share my art and joy through cornhusk doll crafting seminars at the Smithsonian and in my home studio. I try to inspire in my students the same confidence and enthusiasm my mother taught me, and to share with them the thought passed along to me by one collector: 'You're never too old to have a happy childhood.'"

Marilyn Radzat/Molly Kenney

"We call ourselves curators of enchantment," say west coast artists Marilyn Radzat and Molly Kenney. "Our artwork showcases the often-overlooked natural beauty of our own world enhanced and 'magicked' by imagination."

These artists, whose works have been exhibited in many galleries across the country and figure in major collections throughout the world, craft pieces that reflect the seasons in addition to their Father Christmases. They have created their 1ft to 5ft (31cm to 152cm) one-of-a-kind figures since 1982, and together produce a line of elegant dolls which are sold under the name MKR DESIGNS®.

Inspiration for Father Christmas and other work comes from poetry, from found objects in the natural world, from fragments of antique lace or fabric discovered in antique shops. Building on the initial idea, Marilyn sculpts the face, hands and feet individually, then paints each piece with oils. Eyes are hand-blown glass from Germany. Components then go to Molly who creates a posable body built up over a wire armature and covered with hand-stitched fabric. The thrust of the design usually gives the finished figure a strong sense of motion. Molly, who has been sewing and costuming since childhood, draws on her collection of treasured antique silks, velvets and laces to design unique costumes for each MKR DESIGNS® doll. Once a doll is completed and costumed, Marilyn applies her very special collage work, using natural treasures — real hair, fur,

moss, leaves, flowers, antique treasures, a pebble from the beach, a shell from the sea. "The collage elements, in combination with sculpting, painting and costuming, give our work its very special glow of enchantment."

Marilyn Radzat began sculpting about 20 years ago and first tried her hand at doll making a decade later. Her initial exhibit in a San Francisco gallery elicited an overwhelmingly enthusiastic response, so overwhelming, in fact, that she looked for a partner to help with costume design and sewing. In Molly Kenney she found a gifted friend and a compatible associate with whom to form MKR DESIGNS®. Marilyn also creates her own line of one-of-a-kind figures (not necessarily Father Christmases!) and was honored at Disney World's exhibition of master doll makers in 1990. One of nine doll artists selected from a global sample, Disney purchased Marilyn's work and created a special environment in which to display it.

Whether a Father Christmas is a Marilyn Radzat original or a Radzat/Kenney joint creation, each is an "old man of the forest," dressed in antique laces, velvets and furs, with a flowing Icelandic sheep-wool beard. And, by combining studio artifice with nature's own art, each carries the artists' message that enchantment in the full sense of the word is possible in the very real world in which we live our lives.

The Santa Sisters

"They began calling us that for fun at the Toy and Miniature Museum of Kansas City where we help set up the annual Christmas display featuring our Santa and Mama Claus," explained Charlene Westling of Topeka, Kansas. "The name, The Santa Sisters, just stuck!" It stuck for a good reason, since sisters Charlene Westling, Alice Swisher and Virginia Studyvin have for years been gladdening the holiday season with their delightful Santa dolls.

The sisters were born in the 1920s in Pittsburg, Kansas, an old-fashioned mining town where their father was a shovel operator with a seven-day work week. "We were lucky if he had half days off on holidays," Virginia told us, "but the rugged routine didn't stop home from being an unusually happy place for us all. Our parents were wonderful people. Mother was a fine seamstress and decorator; Daddy was an avid reader with a memory that never failed. He was also a wonderful storyteller, and some of our happiest memories are of him reading to us.

"We have all sorts of wonderful memories of home," Virginia continued. "For instance, there was Mother's cedar chest, always a mystery and a delight for me. It was a rare treat to be allowed to explore the contents which included Mama's own childhood dolls, a china head and a bisque-headed baby. Those precious family treasures fascinated me as a child and probably helped form my interest in doll making and collecting."

All three sisters enjoyed art classes in school and studio classes as adults. World War II, marriage and family rearing backburnered the arts for years, but when their children started moving toward independence and careers were steady-state, there was more leisure and together time. "We'd do things together and go places, and on one outing we came across a shop in the Kansas City area that had reproduction dolls in the window with an offer of classes. We have a photo of our mother, aged about three, and have always thought she'd make an adorable doll. But we hadn't the faintest notion how to go about making one. This seemed an ideal place to begin to learn."

The lessons were fun, but once the sisters had mastered basic techniques, they turned their backs on repros to strike out as independents, and Santa Claus was their first original project, commissioned by a lady who planned to open a Santa Museum. "The fantasy of Santa Claus was an important part of our childhood, and the natural choice for a Santa model was our own father," Charlene smiled. "I developed the prototype from family photographs,

allowing myself some artistic license with proportions, but striving to capture his infectious grin, rather pronounced ears and nose and the familiar twinkle in his eyes."

That original Santa, dressed in knickers and vest, was introduced at the 1983 UFDC Regional Conference in Pueblo, Colorado, where he won a blue ribbon in the competition. "We were thrilled and promptly formed a partnership called 'I Believe...'". And that's how we started producing Santas!"

From the beginning, those Santas were immensely popular with collectors, so much so that one year into production Alice sculpted Mama Claus as a companion doll. The demand continued to increase, yet the sisters refused to seek out shortcuts to hurry their work. "It isn't easy to produce enough dolls to satisfy collectors," Alice admits. "We still do every step in the process ourselves and won't compromise on quality. People have to understand that much of the charm of our work relates to its very personal roots, to plenty of 'TLC' in the studio. This is a hobby, a work of love, not a business."

Today, the sisters make two versions of Charlene's original Santa. Both utilize the same basic 15in (38cm) doll with porcelain head, hands and feet and a wood-and-wire armature body. Many of the dolls are costumed in the prize-winning UFDC knickers and vest outfit and hold a pencil in one hand and a long, curling scroll in the other, with "For Good Girls and Boys" calligraphed across the top. "We were delighted when we discovered collectors were inscribing the scroll with a sort of family tree," Charlene said. "Many people fill it with the names of children and grandchildren, which tremendously enhances its personal value."

Dolls not dressed in the UFDC costume wear an outfit that could have been lifted from a 1930s Coca Cola® advertisement, a jolly red wool jacket with trousers and cap to match, properly trimmed with rabbit fur. Santa's belt and boots are genuine kidskin, his hair and whiskers real lambswool. Beneath the jacket, he sports swank Gucci suspenders and cream-colored woolen longjohns (monogrammed!) complete with buttons and stitched drop seat. From start to finish, each doll is lovingly hand-crafted, with Charlene making porcelain components and assembling the wood-and-wire frame for the body, Alice crafting the leather belt and boots and Virginia, who inherited a rare gift for needlework from her talented mother, cutting and sewing all the costumes.

Many of today's top artists permanently affix clothing to their dolls, each of which is conceived as a composition where positioning of accessory objects and drapery of fabrics contribute to a fragile artistic unity. The Santa Sisters, by contrast, see their work as an *active* force in family joy of the season. Their dolls are completely undressable; in fact, the costumes are sold with the dolls or separately, and many collectors purchase one doll with *both* costumes for the pleasure of dressing the doll to suit the occasion.

"We love what we do," Alice Swisher mused, "and although one never knows what the future holds, for us it will most certainly include dolls. They've become quite a family thing, with brothers, nieces, daughter and granddaughters all interested and involved. One little granddaughter tells me 'I'm going to be a doll lady just like you when I grow up, Grandma.' The funny thing is we still haven't done that doll of our little mother. But we will one day, when we're ready."

Judie Tasch

Texas artist Judie Tasch's mother treasures the sock dolls her daughter made as an eighth-grade home economics project. And round the world, serious doll collectors treasure the cloth dolls Judie makes *now* — dolls that eerily echo 19th century work by Ludwig Greiner, Izannah Walker and Martha Chase. This extraordinary artist crafts black dolls and floppy cloth dolls dressed in antique and "antique look" fabrics garnered during weekly forays to the Austin branch of Good Will Industries. Judie's 22in (56cm) Victoria, Nathaniel and Cordelia, as well as 16in (41cm) Baby Mary, have molded cloth faces painted and antiqued by the artist. She also crafts very special Father Christmases that combine her personal art orientation with the best of the old-world folk tradition.

Judie loved dolls intensely throughout her childhood; she played with them and crafted her own. When her sons were small, she made stuffed animals for their nurseries, then went on to design and sew cloth puppets that gave three-dimensional form to the storybook characters that filled their elementary school "readers." When the Tasch's two sons entered high school, their mother used her newfound leisure to further explore the mysteries of doll making. She experimented with porcelain, then switched to cloth, the medium in which she has always felt most comfortable. Her instinct to craft dolls that combine Victorian and folk styles meshed perfectly with the enthusiasm for American folk art and antiques that swept the country during the early 1980s and, from the start, marketing her work posed no problems.

Judie Tasch's Father Christmas dolls share many of the qualities that characterize her cloth "babies." They, too, are reminiscent of an earlier age. Each of the artist's Santas has a wooden body (crafted by Judie's husband), firmly anchored to a 4in by 4in (10cm by 10cm) wooden base. Doll faces are painted fabric treated to resemble leather. "Each face has a center seam nose," Judie told us. "They are old men with wizened, contemplative expressions, blue eyes surrounded by age and smile wrinkles and furrowed brows. I use techniques similar to the ones that bring my other cloth dolls to life when I craft, paint and antique Santa faces," she added. "And every Father Christmas has a beard, hair and moustache of natural uncarded mohair. In fact, I use natural materials almost exclusively for my dolls and Santas."

The artist's Father Christmases are available as limited edition pieces or as one-of-a-kind masterpieces. Sizes range from 6ft (2m) all the way down to 15in (38cm) tall. Judie designs the dolls' costumes which are sewn by a local dressmaker. All painting, finishing and detail assembly are done by Judie herself, who sees her work as complex, three-dimensional studies in period atmosphere, texture, color and design. Brocades, velvets, Sequoia cones, toys in Santa's pack, a birdcage balanced in a mittened hand, a bundle of real switches found in a real woods — all are arranged by the artist with exquisite attention to effect. "The look is natural," Judie explains. "Colors, textures and objects all fit together as in nature. Perhaps the most fascinating challenge I face in the studio comes each time I try to consciously recreate the order in disorder that characterizes the natural world and the best old art tradition. *That* is very, very difficult."

Roberta Taylor

"I grind my own pigments and use only natural materials. No synthetics!" Father Christmas artist Roberta ("Bobbie") Taylor states firmly, adding, "In my work, modern acrylic paint and modelling media like Sculpey® don't express what I want to say." Which is why this amazing Ohio artist, whose Santas made the December covers of *Early American Life* in 1988 and 1990, uses craft techniques akin to those employed by factories, studios and cottage industries a century or more ago. That, plus extraordinary talent and a never-ending quest for old-world legends about the Christmas Man, imbue Bobbie's work with a special magic uniquely its own.

Roberta Taylor's art background is impressive. She studied at the Cleveland Art Institute, specializing in silversmithing and textiles. After graduation, she worked first in the Art Department at American Greetings, then became a freelance artist. She created craft objects, collected and studied antiques and antique fabrics, and worked for decorators for whom she painted *trompe l'oeil*, false graining and wall murals in the 19th-century tradition.

During those early years, Bobbie Taylor was also active in antique repair and restoration and had many opportunities to handle and restore older Santa treasures from private and museum collections. She was soon fascinated by the beauty and intricate construction methods used by the long-ago anonymous artisans whose work she saved. However, the *variety* of Father Christmases mystified her and to better understand the different types, she began collecting old-world Father Christmas legends. "I wanted to learn all the old stories about him," she explained, "and I was startled to discover how difficult it can be to actually pin down local tradition. You think you have it," she grinned. "You've found *the* Latvian Christmas story. And then you discover that what you assumed was a *national* tradition really belongs to a tiny geographic pocket. Over the next hill or across the river the story is different again."

Since there is infinite variety within Father Christmas's story, Bobbie felt free to use artistic license in her studio interpretations of the Christmas Man. She plunged into Father Christmas craft experiments, creating figure after figure, each a stunning blend of old-world Santa lore, traditional Christian iconography and her own very individual artistic thrust.

Bobbie saved her very first Father Christmas project (*Cf.* illustration), a mischievous Santa elf crafted in 1976 as a holiday surprise for her son. This whimsical 10in (25cm) figure sports rabbit fur whiskers and wears the familiar brick red wool felt that typifies old candy container Santas from Germany. In fact, Bobbie's #1 Santa Claus *is* a candy container. His body separates above the clothespin whittled legs to reveal a hollow tube filled with holiday sweets.

Since her early experiments in the 1970s, Roberta Taylor has crafted hundreds of big and little Father Christmases that echo old-world traditional types. Bobbie Taylor Santas include Saints, Moors, elves and gnomes. She makes dour Belsnickles and rotund, grandfatherly Père Noëls. "Every year I try another style Father Christmas," she told us. "In 1990, I had an especially exciting time making my Saint Nicholas with the Infant Jesus in his arms. In that piece, I tried to say it all. The group embraces Christian as well as pagan tradition; it balances the lighted evergreen against the sculpted infant designed in the mood of 18th century crèche art. And the baby holds a globe in one hand, symbolic of His love for all humanity."

Each Roberta Taylor Father Christmas body is a wire armature covered with papier-mâché, then wrapped round with cotton batting. Heads, hands and booted feet are pressed papier-mâché cast in molds crafted by the artist. "I have lots and lots of molds, especially for Father Christmas heads," Bobbie said. "The heads all derive from faces I've really encountered. I look for kind, older faces with lots of wrinkles. Wrinkles can be wonderful; they're the lines of life. Once, at a show, a huge older gentleman with sensational pure white whiskers studied the Santas on my table. He could have been the *real* Father Christmas. He was amazing! One of my favorite molds," she added, "is a wonderful face I found in an antique print years ago. The picture shows an elderly French farmer picking grapes. He looks sad and tired, as though he's finishing a hard day's work."

Bobbie beards her Father Christmases with real fur, but she prefers to *paint* their eyes and eyebrows. "I can make a strong artistic statement with a few good brush strokes," she said. "Carefully delineated eyes and eyebrows add tremendously to the expression of a face. In fact, it may be heretical to say so, but I sometimes wish I didn't need to use fur at all!"

Costumes for Bobbie Taylor's art dolls are as critical to the overall composition as are the faces, clothing and pose of the figures. She possesses a vast collection of fabrics, accessories and trims. "I love to use antique silk velvets to dress many of my Santas," she explained. "Old moth-eaten paisley shawls are real studio finds, too. I cut out the damaged bits and use the rest." Bobbie's small 4½in to

11in (12cm to 28cm) Christmas gnomes (*Cf.* illustrations) wear kitten-soft robes made from old cotton flannel baby blankets. Santa's toys, almost all of which are crafted by the artist, include wonderful jack-in-the-boxes, lambs, pulltoys and dolls.

Iconographic detail includes the lambs, evergreens and holly and the shining stars Bobbie often places on Father Christmas's cap. "I believe this detail has Lithuanian roots," she told us. And what about those wonderful flags that add such character, color and dimension to her work? "I just happen to love flags," Bobbie laughed, "and I include them whenever I have the chance. I have some wonderful antique silk flags, and I look forward to using them all!"

Judi Vaillancourt

Chalkware Santas from Vaillancourt Folk Art™ have become part of the American Christmas. They blend traditional forms with contemporary interpretations and techniques and epitomize the best of today's American craft movement. Behind Vaillancourt's fabulous Santas, who carry packs, trees and switches, ride on sleighs, motorcycles, donkeys and pigs and wear red, blue, green, brown or colorful patterned robes, is brilliant 20th century artist Judi Vaillancourt, her astonishing collection of over 1350 antique metal chocolate and ice cream molds, and an idea.

Judi Vaillancourt was raised in Sutton, Massachusetts, surrounded by the art, antiques and Americana she has loved since childhood. "While other kids were interested in what was new, I was fascinated by the history in older homes and their furnishings," she said. "One of my neighbors had a big old house filled with antiques, and I loved to visit her. Around 14, I began to refinish antique furniture as a hobby."

Judi empathizes with antique furniture and applied art "to an almost uncanny degree," according to her husband and business partner Gary Vaillancourt. It was that empathy that gave her college studies and ultimate professional track direction. She crafted colonial furniture, developed a line of clocks that derive from circa 1700-1750 grandfather clock faces. She painted scenes and portraits, designed and constructed custom fireplace mantels and, around 1984, she began experimenting with antique Father Christmas molds, — she then owned three! Judi tried filling the molds with a wide range of materials, from beeswax to plaster, but the results were unsatisfactory. At last, she tried chalkware, a quick-drying plaster-like substance our Victorian ancestors called "poor man's Staffordshire." Chalkware gave the fine definition of detail she had been seeking, and when Judi's #1 Chalkware Father Christmas, displayed at a local folk art show in 1984, brought home enthusiastic orders for 30 more, Vaillancourt Folk Art was born. At first, Gary Vaillancourt molded the figures himself, putting in long hours every evening after his already long business day as a computer software marketing executive. Judi then painted and finished the pieces in the family's dining room converted to studio/workroom.

In 1986, Vaillancourt Folk Art™ was growing fast, and Gary and Judi became full-time business partners in what is now the nation's largest producer of chalkware figures, particularly Father Christmases. The ground floor of an 1820s Massachusetts farmhouse is given over completely to a showroom for their own and fellow artists' work in the American folk art tradition. The second floor of the farmhouse is a busy chalkware factory staffed by 20 highly-trained artisans who produce 250 different designs each year. Each derives from an antique chocolate or ice cream mold in the Vaillancourts' burgeoning collection. Gary handles the marketing side of the business; Judi does all the designing and paints the prototype figures from which her staff paints and "antiques" signed, numbered and dated limited editions that figure among the country's most sought-after Christmas collectibles.

The antique molds behind Vaillancourt designs have their own exciting tale to tell. Two-piece metal molds for chocolate or, occasionally, for ice cream production, were first made in France around 1850 but by 1900 their manufacture was centered in Germany, where the acknowledged master mold maker was Anton Reiche of Dresden. "To design his magnificent molds," Gary Vaillancourt explains, "Reiche employed the same level of artist and sculptor as those then crafting finely-detailed porcelain and Christmas tree ornaments of the period." After 1880, two metal mold firms were established in New York City, and German firms were represented in our country by agents, particularly by the T.C. Weygandt Co., chief "rep" for Anton Reiche.

Disaster struck German manufacturers when production and exports were halted by World War I. Companies tried to reestablish themselves in postwar Europe, but the depression years cut deeply into sales, and Hitler's rise led to mandated swastika, tank and gun molds that were unmarketable outside Germany. Production once again ground to a complete stop in 1939; Dresden (and with it the Anton Reiche factory) was devastated by Allied bombing raids and, after 1945, old expensive metal molds became white elephants in the new, expanding age of plastics. Master dies were sold as scrap, and today there are only a few European-based companies that continue to produce metal molds. The largest of these is B.V. Vormanfabriek, located in Tilburg, Germany.

Gary Vaillancourt explained how the metal molds for thousands of circa 1850-1900 chocolate Father Christmases were made by old-world craftsmen. "A design was given to an artist, who sculpted a three-dimensional plaster form that was cut in two to create the front and back pieces used to make the master die. Then, liquefied metal (usually an alloy called 'German silver') was poured into a sand casting of the plaster halves to form a rough metal casting from which master male and female dies were made. Rough dies were cleaned and re-etched, if needed, to enhance their detail. To complete the mold," Gary continued, "a metal blank was inserted between the two dies, with varying amounts of pressure applied to achieve the desired shape. The number of times a die was struck depended on the depth of the mold and the amount of detail required. Once they were pressed out of the metal, molds were trimmed and stamped with a style and/or mold number. Then they were tin-plated, stamped with the manufacturer's name or mark and polished."

One looks at photos of pre-1900 German factory workrooms; at the Vaillancourts' marvelous collection of antique tin-plated Santa molds, sole survivors of a unique partnership between industry and art a century or more ago — and at the busy chalkware factory in an old Massachusetts farmhouse, and one cannot help wondering. How much Judi Vaillancourt and the old craftsmen would have to say to one another if they could meet today. And how curious that tin-plated molds designed for the Victorian confectionery trade should become the springboard from which a contemporary artist has launched a new American folk art form. Chalkware replaced chocolate; paint replaced colored foil. The level of workmanship remains first-rate, as is that most popular subject depicted by the old-world mold makers, — Santa Claus!

Rosemary Volpi

Rosemary Volpi is that rare phenomenon, a contemporary artist who has backed away from the rush and push of our 20th century to recreate the slow-paced ambiance of another era, one where she feels at home and lives her own very special artistic experience. With her family roots in Italy, it is no surprise that Rosemary's unique studio world echoes Old Masters paintings and the exquisite sculpture, costumes and accessories that grace the best of 18th-century Neapolitan crèche figures. "I look at pictures of those wonderful pieces and wish I could breathe them in!"

This extraordinary artist, who crafted her first Father Christmas in 1984, was born in Chicago, then raised in southern California. She looks back with nostalgia on a happy childhood in a warm, close-knit family. "I was an only child and spent many hours creating my own little worlds — drawing, crafting furniture for my dollhouse, day dreaming. Artwork and crafts have been important to me for as long as I've known myself."

Those art interests intensified in the years following Rosemary's marriage to Gastone Volpi who was born in Ceprano, Italy. During Italian holidays with her husband, Rosemary divided her time between visits with his family resident abroad, her own family and visits to museums and galleries, where she gained an ever-deeper appreciation of vintage art. "My family and friends have always encouraged me to continue my artwork," she told us, "even during the busy years when we were raising our son,

Joseph. And all the impressions — people, faces, books, places, museums — were stored away in my imagination to reappear in the work I'm doing today."

Those impressions included the discovery that the old-world Father Christmas was a very different person from the Thomas Nast and Sundblom Santa Claus American children grow up with. "I have always loved Christmas and Christmas things, so I was surprised and happy when I learned that the old Father Christmas was a *saintly* soul, that he symbolized benevolence, peace, kindness, every good thing," Rosemary recounted. "That gave me a focus; I decided to combine the love of old-world art and crèche figures with the 'Spirit of the Season,' to create a Father Christmas for my family. It seemed that this would be the ideal gift from my heart."

To prepare herself for crafting that first figure, Rosemary took several classes in doll making. She studied faces and fixed in her mind the features she wanted to model "in order to express my feelings about what Father Christmas actually means to me." Her first piece was dressed in red hopsacking and carried a handmade basket filled to overflowing with toys the artist crafted herself. "It was a wonderful adventure and along the way I discovered many of the studio techniques I still use today. Of course, I've refined my work, but the basics all came together in 1984. To this day, my family and I treasure our #1 Father Christmas. He was my gift of love and we will never part with him."

Eight years and many Father Christmases later, Rosemary's focus remains unchanged. She tries to make each of her holiday figures an embodiment of love and peace, in the hope that it will carry the spirit of goodness which, for her, is Christmas, into the homes of collectors who purchase her work. "She creates her one-of-a-kind pieces slowly," an interviewer wrote several years ago. "She seems to love them into existence."

Rosemary sculpts the head and hands of her Father Christmases in synthetic clay which, after firing and painting, resembles the traditional materials used by the old Italian artists whose work she so admires. Like the old crèche dolls, bodies for her figures are wire armatures wrapped round with batting. Hair, beards, costumes and accessories follow, all predetermined by the idea which inspired the individual piece she is working on.

Each figure and, most particularly, each face, grows first in Rosemary's imagination, and it is this image that she struggles to recapture in clay and fabric. "Most of my figures take a long time to complete," she confessed. "My volume certainly isn't great! I play and play with the clay, the pose, the costume detail. Often, I let figures sit for a long time between work sessions. I come back again and again to study them, make changes, and finally to move forward to the next work stage. Sometimes, when a figure has been left alone for awhile, it seems to take on an identity peculiarly its own and almost tells me what it needs done next."

Nothing is random in this artist's Colorado studio. Everything — expressions, poses, costumes, accessories — all are designed to enhance the feeling and mood she is trying to portray. Whenever possible, she dresses her figures in antique fabrics, trims, laces, buttons and furs. In fact, the discovery of a wonderful old leather belt, marvelous antique pewter buttons or a fine old fabric can trigger an entire project, bring a face and idea into focus. Rosemary also crafts every toy and accessory that spills from the sacks and baskets with which her Father Christmases are loaded. Moravian paper stars, doll size metal horns, teddy bears, lamb pulltoys — she

makes them all and takes tremendous pleasure in this additional studio challenge. She even weaves the baskets her figures carry and enjoys recounting how she learned this traditional craft. "When I was a child," she explained, "my father was a counselor at a summer day camp, and my mother, grandmother and I attended 'craft sessions' there. We had a wonderful time learning to make baskets. All three of us sat at the edge of the children's wading pool where the reed was submerged in water to keep it soft. We laughed, all together there in the warm sunshine, learning how to make baskets..."

In addition to her Father Christmas sculptures, which average 24in (61cm) tall, Rosemary crafts white-clad angel children like those on old greeting cards and Victorian scraps. She also creates gorgeous dollsize angels, with delicately-tinted real feather wings, cousins of the antique figures that float above the crèche in the Medieval Hall of New York's Metropolitan Museum of Art each December.

Perhaps her most unusual piece, a bow to her Italian heritage and very much in the mood of crèche sculpture, is La Befana, a Christmas folk figure out of the artist's south European past. Traditionally, La Befana is depicted as a witch; Rosemary reworked the idea as an Italian peasant woman. According to the old legend, the artist explained, the Magi encountered La Befana on their way to Bethlehem. They asked her to join them on their journey but she hesitated and when, later, she set out to follow them, she lost her way. "So now she wanders the world in search of the Christ Child," Rosemary concluded, "giving presents to good children in the hope that one of them will prove to be Him, and leaving coals in the stockings of the naughty ones."

For Rosemary Volpi, art has brought a double blessing. Her gifts enable her to give material shape to the image which, for her, symbolizes peace, kindness, "all good things." And she has the additional joy of being able to share her very private image of Father Christmas with others. "These two things," she said, "are part of my personal and very special gift from Father Christmas."

Faith Wick

Faith Wick's amazing life, as well as her beautiful doll artistry, have been featured again and again in doll and collector publications. Perhaps the fullest coverage of her story is to be found in Helen Bullard's excellent book, *Faith Wick: Doll Maker Extraordinaire* (Hobby House Press, Inc., 1986), an elegant account of Faith's fascinating real-life and studio adventures.

Faith was born and raised in small Minnesota communities where her artistic precocity was evident from earliest childhood. Looking back, she is amazed to see how many family photographs of herself, both as a girl and as a young adult, include favorite dolls. This empathy for dolls spilled over into classroom teaching before and after her marriage to Melvin Wick. Faith writes of this earliest classroom experience: "My two-year degree for teaching kindergarten gave me the chance to have the same kind of elaborate doll arrangements for the children which I had made for myself as a little girl who played alone much of the time in her large outdoor playhouse. Now, as a kindergarten teacher, I could have a wonderful doll corner for the often-underprivileged children whom I was teaching. I introduced them to a fairytale world of fancy circuses and farms with animals known only in fantasies."

Much of what followed is legendary. Faith and Mel Wick's family grew up. The couple bought Fairyland Park, a down-at-the-heels Minnesota theme park that became their home; Helen Bullard writes: "The family lived in a little fairytale French-style cottage in the park and the children played in the Old Woman's Shoe!" Faith and Mel rolled up their sleeves when the regular business day had ended and began the difficult task of relandscaping the park and repairing the exhibits. Faith admits that she is probably the only doll artist, now or in the past, whose apprenticeship was spent working with life-size cement statues in a fantasy theme park.

By the time the couple gave up Fairyland Park and moved to Grand Rapids, Minnesota, Faith's hands-on education in sculpture and painting was complete. So was her formal schooling, since this ambitious woman had used eight Fairyland Park summers to go back to college, where she earned not one, but two degrees! In Grand Rapids, she missed the large-scale craft work that had been her life in Fairyland Park, so she switched to "small" and started creating the dolls for which she is known today. Among them is a multitude of delightful Father Christmases.

"Over the years, my work divided into three parts," Faith told us. She designed dolls for commercial firms like ENESCO®, Effanbee®, Silvestri® and R. Dakin®. Additionally, from 1978 through the mid-1980s, she ran an extraordinary doll-making business called Wicket Originals, Inc.®, with a total issue of over 600 different dolls. The thousands of craft tasks needed to complete this impressive output were farmed out to cottage industry artisans across the country, front-rank craftspeople Faith had met through the show circuit over the years. Finally, since her election to NIADA in 1978, the artist has developed her own studio art and produced a stunning list of one-of-a-kind or limited edition pieces, each crafted from start to finish by Faith alone.

Pictured here are representative Faith Wick Santas that date from the late 1970s through 1990. Shown are Faith's very first Santa, a wax Santa made ten years later, and assorted pieces from the commercial, Wicket Originals and NIADA work — a studio sampler that illustrates the evolving thrust of this artist's beautiful work.

Kim Bell

Photographs courtesy of Kim Bell

Virginian Kim Bell at work in her 100-year-old home. Her Victorian-style Father Christmases are an outgrowth of the artist's love of Victoriana and period holiday decor.

A white-robed Victorian Father Christmas with a holly wreath, suede toy sack, bunch of switches and an evergreen, a design reminiscent of antique Christmas scraps.

This Victorian Father Christmas wears a hooded, wine-colored woolen coat trimmed with fur. The turned hardwood base is fashioned from pieces of century-old flooring taken from the attic of the Bells' Virginia home!

RIGHT: Each Kim Bell Father Christmas begins as a lump of clay. "I develop the clay into what I feel Father Christmas would look like if we could really see him, complete with wrinkles, smiling eyes and a whimsical expression."

A cheery "hello" from Santa riding in a hardwood sleigh crafted by Kim's talented husband, Mike Bell.

ABOVE LEFT: A rich tumble of whiskers and fur-fringed hood highlight the clear blue glass eyes of this Kim Bell Father Christmas who stirs thoughts of Russia's Father Frost.

A warm, richly clad Old-World Father Christmas. The dark belted coat and fur hat heighten the exotic flavor of Kim's work.

This Santa, dressed in a floor-length fur-trimmed Victorian Father Christmas robe, backpacks an evergreen. His hands are busy with his toy sack and a miniature sleigh by Mike Bell.

William Bezek

Photographs courtesy of William Bezek

California artist William Bezek, whose first Father Christmases sold out in one hour and who has not stopped creating "living" Santas since!

A peek at Will's studio reveals a collection of completed Father Christmas sculptures and a mounted figure waiting to be costumed by the artist.

Renaissance robes threaded with heavy wire and subtly positioned, a wise, careworn face and unusual mounting angle heighten the illusion of life and size of this remarkable 20in (51cm) sculpture.

As with all of William Bezek's Father Christmas sculptures, the strong, self-assured personality of this figure emerged, seemingly from nowhere, as the artist refined and painted the face. Once the personality is clearly defined, Will explained, the figure almost dictates terms to the artist!

An old-world introspective Father Christmas lost in dreams of the past. He wears antique brocade and carries an imitation suede sack, since the artist believes the killing of fur-bearing creatures to satisfy human vanity is at odds with the spirit of the season.

Santa with rocking horse, a fragile figure that seemed to ask for a single toy rather than a heavy sackful. Note the 17th-century buckled shoes and candy-cane-striped "witch's stockings"!

A dynamic Christmas Man wears a wreath of fruit and carries a simple bundle of sticks. This Victorian figure, which echoes the mood, design and palette of 19th-century postcard Santas, is worlds apart from the "Yes, Virginia" Santa Claus we grew up with!

Will's Victorian Santa poses for the camera against a San Francisco Gothic window inset with 19th-century stained glass detail.

Beth Cameron

Photographs by J. W. Photography
Courtesy of Beth Cameron

The Cameron studio provides a fascinating creative atmosphere, with its clutter of props and furnishings, work-in-progress, furs, fabrics, accessories and fabulous view of western Pennsylvania woodlands.

A magnificent seated Santa, 17in (43cm) tall, is surrounded by elegant accessories that include an antique toy tree, toys and old and new hand-crafted furniture. Beth conceives each grouping as a complex work of art in which positioning of figures and objects contribute to the total composition.

Jolly Santa, a 1987 design, is among Beth's favorites. The 15in (38cm) figure wears a wool and leather outfit with antique pewter buttons. His foaming whiskers are newborn lambswool.

Jolly Santa (detail) reveals the artist's sensitive sculpture. "I find the lines and wrinkles of age fascinating. They are character lines, the record of living."

Beth believes hands express character just as faces do. She begins each Santa project by sculpting the head and hands for her new figure.

A 20in (51cm) Father Christmas in the Russian mood poses in a wintry land-scape framed by antique toy fencing. His fur, like that used for all Beth's creations, is "recycled."

An assemblage of Beth Cameron Santas wear costumes ranging from a Victorian Father Christmas (left) to the hardworking Mr. Claus (right).

A 1987 piece Beth calls Off-Season Santa. The apron is antique linen, hand-woven a century ago from flax grown on Beth's grandfather's farm. Santa's beard is lambswool, and the tartan sack started life as a 19th-century Scottish shawl.

Grand Santa. Note the sensitively sculpted face with its very human expression and wrinkles the artist calls the "lines of living." Beth's 1988 one-of-a-kind Grand Santa stands 22in (56cm) tall. The face, framed by goat fur whiskers, lacks the traditional moustache. "I mind covering a finely-detailed face with all that fur and was delighted to discover collectors are just as pleased with my work when Santa is bald and clean shaven!"

Detail of Beth's seated 18in (46cm) Father Christmas. The artist feels "that most doll makers give their creations eyes that are all wrong. Human eyes are comparatively small in the face and never totally open," she explained. "The lines of lids and brows contribute to the overall expression of a living face."

Beth's marvelous 1991 black Santa loaded with presents that include a delightful teddy bear, a red wagon, books and a black dollie. Is the bike for a good little boy? Or is it this Santa's update of the old-fashioned sleigh and eight tiny reindeer!

A group composed of Father Christmas, Beth's "children" and wonderful accessories. The artist is fascinated by complex compositions in which every article of clothing, figure and accessory is deftly positioned to contribute to the total impact.

Lois Clarkson
Photographs courtesy of Lois Clarkson

Lois poses outside her Pennsylvania studio with a life-size English Father Christmas dressed in a *real antique Father Christmas robe and hat!*

RIGHT: A German Father Christmas, 3ft (1m) tall, rides an antique sled. The figure wears antique children's shoes and carries toys that include a straw-stuffed primitive elephant.

BELOW: Lois's delightful "Santa's Santa," a virtuoso piece 4ft (122cm) tall, loaded with real antique Santa dolls!

Detail of *"Santa's Santa."*

Lois's English
Victorian Father
Christmas in
vintage Santa
robe and hat
poses alone
outside Snowdin
Studios. The
antique costume
did not include
footwear, so Lois
improvised with
her daughter's old
paddock boots.
"My husband had
to cut through the
steel heels to
attach the figure to
its wooden base!"

Close-up of Lois's 4ft (122cm) Santa dressed in an antique burgundy velvet suit.

Jolly American Coca-Cola® Santa from the 1940s, the Santa type Lois grew up with!

A rosy, windblown Father Christmas keeping warm under a cozy fur hood. Detail of a 3½ft (1m, 15cm) figure riding a small antique sled from northern New England. The sled formerly did service to transport buckets of maple syrup.

This traditional German Father Christmas from the Black Forest carries an antique basket that contains an antique straw-stuffed Steiff dog, an old cloth book and child's coat, an old toy tennis racket and an antique composition doll with a straw-stuffed body and arms attached with metal pins.

A 30in (76cm) Victorian Father Christmas backpacking a tree richly decorated with antique tinsel and topped with an old tinsel star.

Canadian artist Janice Crawley poses beside the family Christmas tree in chilly Winnipeg!

Janice Crawley
Photographs courtesy of Janice Crawley

RIGHT: Wouldn't Beatrix Potter laugh if she could see Tom Kitten wearing this jolly red velvet Santa suit! Soft-toy Thomas is 7in (18cm) tall with real glass cat eyes. *Photograph by Peter Groesbeck.*

BELOW: Janice Crawley's high-fashion soft toy pig Santa Claus wears a red velvet suit neatly belted in black leather. This whimsical 10in (25cm) fellow lugs a drawstring sack stuffed with real candy canes and toys, including a teeny tiny porcelain googly made by the artist. *Photograph by Peter Groesbeck.*

Janice's warmly-dressed shy Santa bear is 6½in (16cm) tall, made of fur fabric and fully jointed. *Photograph by Peter Groesbeck.*

This 1¾in (5cm) tiny may just be the world's smallest artist quality Santa Claus! Crafted of porcelain and fabric by Canadian artist Janice Crawley, whose virtuoso talent (she can do anything!) is featured again and again in these pages. *Photograph by Peter Groesbeck.*

A dollhouse-scale Santa with modeled (not molded) Fimo® head, delicately painted features and stuffed cloth body. Red suit and black boots are velvet. Teddy, clown and doll in Santa's sack are by the artist. *Photograph by Peter Groesbeck.*

An old-fashioned Father Christmas with a European flavor, 12in (31cm) tall, carries a staff, tree, toy sack and basket. This figure has a beeswax-over-wood face. Among the "goodies," he carries a wee doll of porcelain, also from Janice's studio. *Photograph by Peter Groesbeck.*

Piggy Santa and Rabbit Claus are among Janice's jointed all-porcelain "tinies." Rabbit Claus is astonishingly detailed at 1⅛in (3cm) tall. *Photograph by Peter Groesbeck.*

Janice's porcelain-headed teddy bear and kitty Santas. "I'd had the idea for these 'tinies' in my head for years," the artist told us. "The *Santa Dolls* book project gave the extra push to sit down and *make* the dolls." Teddy is 1⅜in (3cm) tall. *Photograph by Peter Groesbeck.*

Glenda Fletcher

Photographs courtesy of Glenda Fletcher

Cloth doll artist Glenda Fletcher caught by the candid camera in a relaxed moment during a 1990 show break!

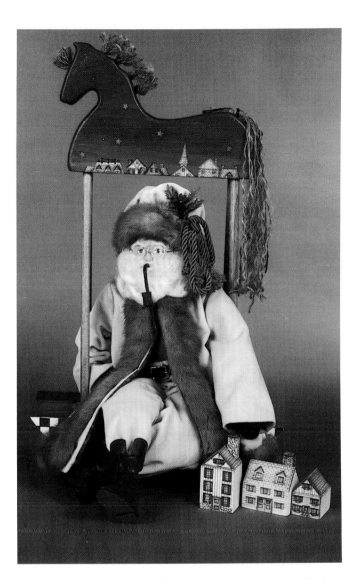

Glenda Fletcher calls her Santas "rag dolls — sort of." One glance at this contemplative Father Christmas seated beneath an elegant blue sky-rocking horse is enough to convince serious collectors that he is far more than that!

Glenda's dolls have hand-sculpted cotton muslin faces and painted features. "If my Santa's face doesn't look back at the person smiling into it, then it's not my doll at all. It's just a handful of stuffing and cloth," the artist says firmly.

Whittler Wally Trott ("he lives just down the road from our house") crafts the hands and feet Glenda attaches to her dolls. Every pair of hands and feet are different and, according to the artist, they get better and better.

To Glenda, Santa looks like a father, an uncle, a neighbor. She dresses her dolls in the kind of clothes she is familiar with. "I can't imagine Santa Claus dressed any other way."

Glenda's "down home" Santa, with pipe and suspenders, shares a quiet moment with collectors.

Glenda's soft, lovable Santas are individuals, never numbered editions. "How can you put a *number* on Santa Claus!" Costumes are all-natural fabrics — vintage furs and homespuns.

One of Glenda's lovable Santas rocks an adorable cuddly friend. The rocking chair is made to her special order by Maine artist Sharon Tilton. Note the realistic hands whittled by Wally Trott. *Photograph courtesy of Glenda Fletcher.*

No matter the costume or the accessories, Glenda's Santas are warm and open like the artist who makes them. "Santa Claus symbolizes the joyous spirit of Christmas. I make Santas to help keep that spirit alive all through the year."

Artist Judy Fresk poses for the camera in her Connecticut studio.

Judy Fresk
Photographs courtesy of Judy Fresk

Judy's best-selling piece, her Elizabethan Father Christmas with tree is a dream fantasy of Renaissance exotica that belies the dull truth of 16th/17th century European Reformation history. In actual fact, there was little seen of the "Christmas Man" during the somber years that followed Luther's challenge to the traditional Church.

A Victorian Gift Giver in the English mood. Note Judy's effective use of baskets imported from India. Accessories, fabrics and trim are all contemporary materials adapted by the artist for a vintage look.

A "Clement Moore Gift Giver" that echoes the future of America's Santa Claus tradition. The 18in (46cm) piece is one of an edition of 1500.

ABOVE RIGHT: Judy's interpretation of Saint Basil, the Greek Saint whose day (January 1st) is marked by gift giving and feasting. On Saint Basil's Eve, the traditional *Vassilopitta* (Saint Basil's Pie) is cut, and whoever gets the slice containing a hidden coin will have luck through the New Year!

This one-of-a-kind Gift Giver, 26in (66cm) tall, wears a costume designed from antique fabrics and accessories. Judy develops these figures as studies in design, incorporating color, form, textiles and subtly-positioned accessory detail. Note the marvelous old purse that serves as a sack for this "Christmas Man."

A blue-clad Gift Giver composition. The dramatic costume, like many designed by this artist, began life as an Edwardian blouse! Judy recycles such shirred and tucked treasures, cutting them up and reshaping them as doll costumes. Most of the toys in Judy's Santa sacks are hand-carved by North Carolina artist Ruth Garrison.

ABOVE LEFT: A marvelous Gift Giver in the Russian mood. Note the straight whiskers which contribute to the Eastern look, also the subtle choice of vintage accessories — the beaded purse, old pendant with chain, velvets and gold decorative trim. *Photograph courtesy of Judy Fresk.*

An outstanding example of work from Judy's Connecticut studio, this one-of-a-kind Father Christmas composition includes an antique toy wagon.

Lynn Haney
Photographs courtesy of Lynn Haney

Lynn's 16in (41cm) Russian fantasy Father Frost with Swan Sleigh. The artist hand sculpted the prototype figure and sleigh and designed all costuming and accessorizing.

Detail of Lynn's Woodland Santa. The face is cast in wood composition from a prototype hand sculpted by the artist. "We use wood composition because it provides an especially nice surface for painting," Lynn told us.

Two 18in (46cm) limited edition pieces by Lynn Haney, one a Victorian Father Christmas with Lantern, the other Lynn's Jolly Old Santa.

An 18in (46cm) Victorian Father Christmas with Goose limited edition from Lynn Haney's Texas studios. The figure combines the solemnity of old-world German Santas with the holly wreath and elegant robe of England's Christmas Man.
BELOW: Detail of Illustration at left.

Detail of Jolly Old Santa, red-cheeked and charming in warm velvet, white fur, billowing whiskers and black woolen mittens. "I love to sculpt hands," the artist said, "but sometimes the design really calls for mittens."

Variation on a beloved theme — Lynn's Jolly Old Santa, seated and bespectacled. Is he thinking about prior visits to the good boys and girls on that calligraphed list?

Lew and Barbara Kummerow

Photographs courtesy of Lew Kummerow

Lew's reproduction circa 1910 German candy container Santa-with-Lights is 10in (25cm) tall and makes grudging concessions to the 1990s. Santa's lantern and goose feather tree include four 12 volt battery-operated electric lights!

Adorable small Santa clutching a sprig of lycopodium reproduces a German figure from 1920. This charming 5in (13cm) fellow is structurally as well as visually identical to the antique prototype. *Photograph by Peter Groesbeck.*

A candy container Santa-with-Sleigh and Reindeer, circa 1920, crafted from wood, cloth and plaster. "The slide shows the antique original because Lew hadn't finished his repro in time," Barbara Kummerow confided, adding, "It hardly matters. The antique piece and Lew's copy are virtually indistinguishable from one another!" *Photograph by Peter Groesbeck.*

A 10½in (27cm) standing Santa-with-Basket reproduces a circa 1910-1920 German original. Everything — the heavy wire armature and molded plaster components that form the doll, the felt and flannel clothing and the rabbit fur whiskers — is identical to materials used by the German craftsman who made the prototype nearly a century ago. *Photograph by Peter Groesbeck.*

Old German Santa-with-Sleigh and Horse pull toy 13in (33cm) long and 8in (20cm) high. Like the antique Lew worked from, the sleigh is made from wood and luffa sponge. Horses are papier-mâché with wooden legs. The platform is wood.

Lew's reproduction circa 1930 Japanese Santa-with-Airplane, made from cardboard and cotton batting with pipe cleaner legs. *Photograph by Peter Groesbeck.*

A magnificent one-of-a-kind reproduction by Lew of the rare Althof-Bergmann Santa-with-Sleigh pulled by goats. Copied from an antique example that dates from the 1880s, everything — the tin goats, Santa with his plaster face, cotton gloves and crèpe paper outfit — replicates the mood and texture of the prototype. The pull toy measures 9in by 18in (23cm by 46cm).

ABOVE: Assorted in-scale roly dolls for the dollhouse nursery reproduced from full-size Victorian prototypes. The tiny Santa in front of the bench is an antique reproduction candy container ¾in (2cm) high. Like the prototype, it is hollow and ready to be filled with holiday sweets, if collectors can locate goodies tiny enough to stuff into it! *Photograph by Peter Groesbeck.*

Another repro by Lew of a circa 1930s Japanese charmer. Santa is 2in (5cm) tall with pipe cleaner legs. *Photograph by Peter Groesbeck.*

Question: "When is a doll not a doll?" *Answer:* "When it's a candy container!" This Lew Kummerow original, with its wood box and rabbit fur whiskers, is crafted in the mood of the highly-prized German antiques from the turn of the century. *Photograph by Peter Groesbeck.*

Deborah Lange-Henderson

Photographs courtesy of Debbie Henderson, Henderson Studios Ltd.

Debbie poses for the camera, surrounded by Santas, Mrs. Santa (Settia) and, at the right, her 6ft (2m) Nicholas!

RIGHT: A pair of whimsical 49in (124cm) Santas from 1987 wear startling French tapestry costumes. Their coats are trimmed with brass bells and each is mounted on a walnut base. "We call these guys 'floor Santas!'" Debbie told us with a grin.

Aboard this antique German farm wagon are Debbie's 1990 pack of puckish elves, along with Grand-Père and Nicholas.

A Henderson Studios' Santa party! Back row: 1989 Kris Kringle, a white-robed 1987 Santa trimmed in 14K gold, garnets and German trim, 51in (127cm) tall, and a burgundy velveteen Nicholas with suede boots and a fox-trimmed hat. Front row: Sleeping Nicholas and one-of-a-kind master edition Saint Nicholas in traditional bishop's robes trimmed with 14K gold, European trim and semi-precious stones.

Samples from the artist's private collection include a 33in (84cm) Nicholas playing the violin and a pair of delightful Henderson elves.

Magnificent walking Nicholas braves a winter storm. The figure wears a hand-woven raw silk jacket and Loden green imported wool trousers and hat. Trim includes handmade baskets loaded with greenery and cinnamon sticks.

A 6ft (2m) Spirit of Christmas lives in the Henderson's living room year round. Of course he is laughing! Debbie made him as the model for the jacket photo of her 1990 Santa book.

Thomas Nast would not believe this fabulous *Tibetan-style* Nicholas mounted on a reindeer, a one of a kind masterpiece whose costume includes curly-toed shoes, French ribbons and German trim. The reindeer is hand-carved by Kansas artist Brad Nicholas(!). The saddle is Tibetan sheepskin adorned with ribbons and bells. The figure measures 23in (58cm) tall.

Jocelyn Mostrom

Photographs by R. Tucker Mostrom
Courtesy of Jocelyn Mostrom

Russia's Father Christmas is "D'Yed Moroz" (Father Frost), here shown with his little granddaughter, Snegurochka, The Snow Maiden.

OPPOSITE PAGE: The Mostrom family's full-size Christmas tree features Santas from several studios. In addition to Jocelyn's work, a Father Christmas by Rosemarie Snyder stands beside the large rocking horse; a glorious seated Father Christmas robed in white by Marjorie Van Ditto has an up-front place of honor, and, at the right, stands an old-world type Santa from Deal Dolls in Ohio.

Jocelyn's porcelain and cornhusk 11in (28cm) Saint Nicholas with little Holly and Michael, each 6in (15cm) tall.

A gorgeous 11in (28cm) tall Renaissance angel with a porcelain face. The fragile figure, with its halo and wings, is mounted on a self stand and carries a delicate brass censer.

Saint Lucia wears her traditional holiday crown of candles and is about to carry early morning Saint Lucy cakes to sleeping family members.

ABOVE LEFT: Jocelyn's 9in (23cm) Santa Claus whose costume *and face* are made from cornhusks.

A cornhusk-clad Woodland Santa from Jocelyn's Maryland studio. The piece is inspired by Black Forest traditions.

A limited edition cornhusk Sinterklaas, the Pennsylvania Dutch Father Christmas figure, rides past a pair of delighted cornhusk-clad youngsters.

Jocelyn's "Santa Claus with Sleigh" filled with holiday toys. Santa's face is porcelain with a mohair beard. He wears a cornhusk costume and drives a team of eight delightful reindeer, of which two are shown.

Marilyn Radzat
Molly Kenney

Artist Marilyn Radzat pauses for a moment in the busy California studio where she creates Father Christmases and other display figures that carry her special message to galleries and collections across the country. *Photograph courtesy of Marilyn Radzat.*

Detail of a large, joyous Father Christmas inspired by seemingly humble treasures — a piece of old lace, a remnant of red fabric, a sprig of evergreen, holly berries... Marilyn's art dolls include frequently-overlooked treasures from the past or from nature. She hopes that by "showcasing" such deceptively simple objects, the viewer will develop a keener appreciation of the natural beauty around us — a first step toward preserving it! *Photograph courtesy of Marilyn Radzat.*

A powerful 3ft (1m) tall fur-clad Santa, one of Marilyn Radzat's "enchantment" sculptures, carries treasures we tend to overlook in our hurried lives — exquisite plant forms, a stick... *Photograph courtesy of Marilyn Radzat.*

A gorgeous 3ft (1m) Father Christmas. Like all of this artist's one-of-a-kind sculptures, the figure, with its hand-blown German glass eyes, delicately modeled features, elaborate robes and Icelandic sheep wool hair and beard, is only the raw canvas upon which Marilyn positions treasures from nature. *Photograph courtesy of Marilyn Radzat.*

A 2½ft (76cm) Father Christmas composition from the combined studios of Marilyn Radzat and her needle-artist associate, Molly Kenney. As with all MKR DE-SIGNS® projects, Marilyn sculpted head and hands and created the wire armature body structure. Molly Kenney designed and hand sewed the complex costume and Marilyn applied the finishing collage detailing. *Photograph courtesy of MKR DESIGNS®.*

The Santa Sisters

Photographs by Thad Allton.
Courtesy of "I Believe..."

Alice Swisher, the oldest Santa sister, designed Mama Claus and makes all leather components for the "I Believe" dolls.

Virginia Studyvin, shown dressing Santa (note the monogrammed long-johns!) Virginia sews all costumes for Santa and Mama Claus.

Charlene Westling, who does all sculpting and porcelain painting for Santa and Mama Claus. She designed the original Santa doll the sisters now offer in either of two costumes.

Charlene's original Santa placed first at the 1983 UFDC Regional Conference in Pueblo, Colorado. Today, Virginia costumes some Santas in the 1983 prize-winning outfit designed by Charlene, others in full dress traditional kit sewn and designed by herself.

"Santa's face was inspired by photos of our father," Charlene told us. "Proportions aren't lifelike, but I strove to capture his infectious grin, the twinkle in his eyes, his rather pronounced ears and nose."

BELOW LEFT: The Santa Sisters' Christmas Man in full dress glory — a suit of Pendleton wool with rabbit fur trim, handmade spectacles with nickel silver wire frames and kidskin boots and belt. Beneath all this traditional elegance, Santa wears monogrammed woolly longjohns with an old-fashioned drop seat!

Mama Claus is Alice's original design. She also designed Mama's costume which is handmade by sister Virginia.

Judie
Tasch

Photographs courtesy
Judie Tasch

OPPOSITE PAGE: Judie Tasch crafts 16in (41cm) — life-size Santas in her Austin, Texas, studio. This fellow is life-size, with natural mohair whiskers and a costume that is a typical Tasch interaction of old and antiqued new materials. Note the holly, the bundle of switches, bird cage and cloth toys.

Back view of the life-size Santa shown on opposite page. A marriage of folk art, fine art and whimsy that includes natural woodland elements, dolls, a "goose a-laying" and more.

Another impressive life-size Father Christmas by Judie Tasch. The carved wooden body with its painted, molded cloth face becomes a three-dimensional collage constructed around texture, color, contrast and form.

Judie's Father Christmas figures hint at the unselfconsciousness of 19th-century folk art, while they embody all the elements of carefully composed, very sophisticated contemporary multi-media sculptures.

BELOW LEFT: A one-of-a-kind Judie Tasch Father Christmas dressed in a fabulous antique crazy quilt trimmed with real fur. The body is wood; the face is sculpted cloth handpainted by the artist. Judie's custom figures measure 20in to 30in (51cm to 76cm) tall.

A 1990 special edition limited to 30 pieces. The 20in (51cm) Father Christmas has a sculpted and painted cloth face with mohair wool beard. His robe is fashioned from a handmade cotton patchwork quilt. The burlap sack overflows with toys, among which are a rag doll, a train, a wheel toy, miniature book, Christmas stocking and a rocking horse.

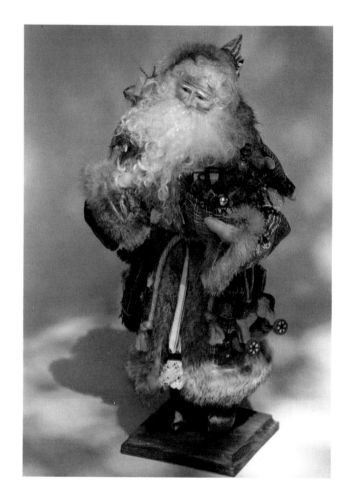

Roberta Taylor
Photographs by Matt Dilyard.
Courtesy of Roberta Taylor

In December 1988, *Early American Life* magazine featured this fantasy Father Christmas from Roberta's Ohio studio on its holiday cover. Like every piece she crafts, this stunning figure echoes Santas of the past filtered through the artist's vivid imagination. He wears stripes and paisleys and packs a fabulous assortment of holiday toys and symbols.

This Father Christmas is an old-world Moor, 18in (46cm) tall, a spin-off of the Black Peter tradition. Note the *painted* eyebrows, wild whiskers, sharp reds and greens of his costume, the jack-in-the-box. Everything contributes to the sheer force of the composition.

A coven of mysterious Christmas Men surprised in an old-world woodland glen. The artist designed these "tinies" to perch on holiday shelves and candle stands. The white-robed gnome at front, center, is 4½in (12cm) high.

OPPOSITE PAGE: At first glance, this 24in (61cm) jolly Santa has the comfortable look of the 1930s/ 1940s Coca-Cola® posters so many of us grew up with. But look again. His costume, with its stripes and paisleys, is unlike any Coca-Cola® Santa and, instead of a sleigh, he sits on a birch log. This figure was the December 1990 cover of *Early American Life*.

This old-world holiday gnome is the first Santa Roberta ever made. He stands about 10in (25cm) tall and wears wool felt, with rabbit fur whiskers. Legs and feet are whittled from a clothespin.

A closer look at the white-robed Christmas gnome featured in the above illustration. This quaint fellow, seated on a traditional birch log, wears a robe sewn from old cotton flannel baby blankets!

A masterful statement of the *full* meaning of Christmas, this other-worldly Saint Nicholas in soft brown robes and Bishop's miter supports the infant Jesus on one arm and carries a lighted evergreen in his free hand. The Holy Infant holds a globe — symbolic of His love for all humanity.

ABOVE LEFT: This is about as close as Bobbie Taylor gets to actually reproducing antique figures. This Father Christmas derives from the German candy container tradition. He *is* a candy container; he separates at the boots and has a holly-paper-covered hollow tube beneath his red robes.

Roberta's completely original Belsnickles derive from antique pieces in her personal collection. The "mica flakes" are *real* antique mica.

The old mold makers capitalized on the variety of transport
vehicles assigned to Santa by
different eras and cultures.
Aside from the sleigh, he has
traveled by goat-drawn wagon,
on the back of a husky pig and,
as illustrated by this poignant
6½in (17cm) repro, on the back
of a truculent mule.

A droll 8½in (22cm) gnome-form Father Christmas lugging a bright red toy sack. The chalkware piece is pictured beside the antique German mold from which it was cast.

ABOVE LEFT: A sampling of pre-World War I molds, the design source for chalkware Santas by Vaillancourt Folk Art™. These two-part "German silver" molds plated with tin served the chocolate and ice cream industries until the advent of plastics made them obsolete. The largest figure pictured is 16in (41cm) tall.

An unusual 12in (31cm) Vaillancourt Father Christmas released in 1990, shown with the antique German mold from which it was cast. Each three-dimensional chocolate or ice cream mold has a back and front with clip closures.

A complicated chalkware group shown with the antique chocolate mold from which the piece was cast. Chalkware sets quickly; after unmolding, the white figure is painted and treated with an "antique" finish in the Vaillancourt workrooms.

Vaillancourt's whimsical green Father Christmas with one hand deep in his pocket, the other holding an oversize sack containing a Noah's Ark.

x

131

Rosemary Volpi

Christmas doll artist *par excellence* Rosemary Volpi poses in her Colorado studio with her enchanting Christkind. Note the angel in flight at top right. *Photograph courtesy of Rosemary Volpi.*

"Santa in The Moon," inspired by an antique postcard from the collection of Beverly Port. This fantasy measures an impressive 32in (81cm) across. In addition to Santa, Rosemary crafted the moon and all the toys in the ensemble. *Photograph by Almida Photography. From the collection of Debbie Masters.*

Again inspired by an antique postcard, Rosemary's brown-robed Father Christmas offers an apple to a studio-crafted goat. As with Saint Francis, Rosemary believes Santa's goodness attracts the creatures of the fields. Hence, the presence of Christmas robins in the setting. *Photograph by Almida Photography. Courtesy of Rosemary Volpi.*

OPPOSITE PAGE: The artist's interpretation of the traditional patron Saint of children, the gift bearer who still visits The Netherlands in these flowing robes each December. *Photography by Almida Photography. Courtesy of Rosemary Volpi.*

It is hard to believe that Rosemary works in the 20th century. Here, the exquisite lamb, the rough-cut metal lantern and the "snow crystals" that highlight Father Christmas's hood, beard and eyebrows contribute to the timeless quality of this ensemble and give it the power of an Old Master's painting. *Photograph by Almida Photography. Courtesy of Rosemary Volpi.*

A green-robed old-world Father Christmas who carries fruit and holiday loaves in addition to toys for all good children. *Photograph by Almida Photography. Courtesy of Rosemary Volpi.*

A blend of symbols enriches this Father Christmas, with his long blue coat, stocking cap and wooden shoes. Rosemary made all the toys as well as the little red hearts that hang from Santa's belt. "I love this piece," she told us. "It's something I saw in my mind's eye and just *had* to create." *Photograph by Almida Photography. Courtesy of Rosemary Volpi.*

A Victorian white-robed Father Christmas derived from a marvelous antique German scrap. He brings lots of toys and carries paper Moravian Christmas stars, symbolic of the Star of Bethlehem. *Photograph by Almida Photography. Courtesy of Rosemary Volpi.*

The symbolic gift giver of Italy, La Befana, is dear to the hearts of all who, like Rosemary and her family, have Italian roots. According to the old story, La Befana refused to follow the Magi and now wanders the earth in search of the Christ Child, giving gifts to good children and leaving coals in the stockings of naughty ones. *Photograph by Almida Photography. Courtesy of Rosemary Volpi.*

ABOVE LEFT: Washington Irving's tongue-in-cheek Dutch Saint Nick rendered exactly as Irving described him in *Knickerbocker's History of New York* published nearly two centuries ago. Note the low, broad-brimmed hat, Flemish trunk hose and tiny windmill. According to Irving, this gentleman flew over the treetops in a horsedrawn wagon to bring gifts to the red-cheeked youngsters of New Amsterdam! *Photograph by Almida Photography. Courtesy of Rosemary Volpi.*

An angel with delicately tinted feather wings from Rosemary's Colorado studio. Enamored by the 18th-century Neapolitan angels that contribute so much to the annual Christmas display at New York's Metropolitan Museum of Art, Rosemary keeps "trying and trying" to recapture the essence of a bygone art form. *Photograph courtesy of Rosemary Volpi.*

In this 1983 photograph, the artist poses with three Wicket Original Father Frosts, all from the same mold. The center figure is dressed in a coat made entirely of real fur.

Faith Wick

Photographs courtesy of Faith Wick

Faith's very first Santa doll, a 1978 Wicket Original she called "Modern Santa."

Faith injects humor into her art. Here are two versions of her "Father" Christmas. At the left, the artist's prototype; at the right, Sylvestri's commercial rendering. The mask motif appears again and again in Faith's doll artistry.

ABOVE LEFT: Ten years after crafting her first Santa Claus, Faith made this wax Santa with glass eyes, wax head and hands and velvet suit. The leather belt and shoes as well as the wooden buttons are handcrafted.

A group of 1989 pieces made for ENESCO®. The large figure at right is a mechanical. Wind him up and he bows from the waist.

A 1986 Wicket Original Scandinavian Santa made from a mold the artist used for Neiman Marcus, Silvestri® and Effanbee®. Scarf, hat and socks are handknits. Boots were a gift from the owner of the Chippewa Shoe Company which outfits travelers to the Arctic. "I thought it fitting that a Lapland Santa should wear them to keep his feet warm," Faith laughed.

ABOVE RIGHT: Faith's marvelous 1986 Scandinavian gnome, a Wicket Original, wears clogs from Sweden and a handwoven shirt trimmed with handwoven braid. Hat is pieced leather; buttons are wood, and he carries another pair of those wonderful snowshoes.

A one-of-a-kind NIADA gift giver, from Faith's brilliant International Gift Giver series begun in 1990. Here, Finland's Joulu Pukki carries his nation's flag and assorted miniature treasures from Finland collected by the artist and her husband.

Again from Faith's Gift Giver series, a Julenissen from Norway. Like other dolls in this group, the Julenissen is a one-of-a-kind NIADA sculpted piece made from clay. Subjects were demonstration models in sculpture classes given by the artist.

Santa Claus in the Dollhouse

Santa porcelains by Virginia master miniaturist Ron Benson. From left: German Santa 1in (3cm) tall, adapted from a circa 1889 glass miniature; small blue Santa with sack, ⅝in (2cm) tall, from a full-size American piece, circa 1860 (exclusive to The Enchanted Doll House); Santa in chimney, ⅞in (2cm) high, based on 1880s illustration by Thomas Nast; American Santa, circa 1880, designed from an antique chocolate mold; Santa candlestick, circa 1880, adapted from a full-size Pennsylvania Dutch chocolate mold. The figure holds an evergreen in its right hand and a bag of coal in its left. *Photograph by Peter Groesbeck. Courtesy of Ron Benson, Richmond, Virginia.*

A group of upstate New York miniaturist Gail Morey's realistic dogs for the dollhouse brighten the holidays and add that nip of chaos that means a true-blue party! From left, back row: seated schnauzer, West Highland terrier, Benji. Front row: wire-haired fox terrier, reclining schnauzer. *Photograph by Peter Groesbeck. Courtesy of Gail Morey.*

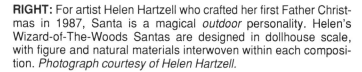

A 6in (15cm) Jolly Santa by Canadian Janice Crawley poses beside the author's cigar box toy shop filled with work by many of today's leading miniaturists. Included are dolls and toys by Eric Horne, Joe Hermes, Swallowhill, the Kummerows, Sue Rountree, Dave Krupick, Fred Laughon, Maggie Anderson, Barbara Raheb, Suzan Kruger and Frances Armstrong. *Photograph by Peter Groesbeck.*

RIGHT: For artist Helen Hartzell who crafted her first Father Christmas in 1987, Santa is a magical *outdoor* personality. Helen's Wizard-of-The-Woods Santas are designed in dollhouse scale, with figure and natural materials interwoven within each composition. *Photograph courtesy of Helen Hartzell.*

From Dorothy Hoskins' Alaska Studio. What fun to surprise Santa catching 40 winks in your very own living room! And he's so-o-o weary that the presence of three bouncy Eskimo children, a baby and a grandma cannot wake him up. *Photograph by Pauline Chamness. Courtesy of We-Two Miniatures.*

A 1984 1/12th scale Santa by Mary Hoot. This multi-media dollhouse artist advertises "No Two Alike," and she means it. *Photograph by Jean Morgan. Courtesy of Mary Hoot.*

Sylvia Lyons' 1984 traditional German St. Nick for the dollhouse is 7in (18cm) tall with working joints and a swivel head. Like other Father Christmases from her studio, the freestanding figure is supported by a cleverly designed and nearly invisible rod and stand. *Photograph by Peter Groesbeck. Courtesy of Sylvia Lyons.*

Sylvia Lyons' larger-than-life-size porcelain Paisley Saint Nick created in 1989, is a towering 7in (18cm) tall! This gorgeous, posable rendering of the immortal Christmas Man has six working joints and a swivel head. *Photograph by Peter Groesbeck, Courtesy of Sylvia Lyons.*

Small-scale Christmas in the dollhouse can be a very grand affair as, depending on the vintage and décor of your mini mansion, cottage or condo, the holidays provide an occasion for infinitely-varied frills and fun. Create a Norman Rockwell down home family Christmas; a Victorian bash complete with roast goose and brandied pudding bursting with raisins and topped with holly; a medieval "groaning board" piled high with suckling pig, swan, meat pasties and fantasy confections. Any and all variations and permutations of our favorite winter setting are realizable in today's fabulous miniature world.

Apart from 1in (3cm)-scale holiday feasts in Fimo®, Sculpey® or porcelain, today's master miniatures artists offer a full range of holly and pine cone wreaths, pine branches to deck the mantel and twist round the stair rail, wrapped and unwrapped gift boxes and every size and sort of Christmas tree, from goosefeather to spruce, to dress up an 1860s parlor or enhance a 1990s high-rise living room. Trees come ready-decorated or ready for you to decorate, drawing on an exquisite array of available in-scale handicrafts — rainbow-hued tree ornaments, paper, berry and popcorn chains, glittering tinsel — delectable miniaturizations in glass, plastic, synthetic clay, wood and paper of the myriad little things that symbolize Christmas.

When full-size Santa dolls, old German candy container treasures and molded chalkware figures are dusted and set out on windowsill, mantel and sideboard in the *real* home each December, similar items are set out in the dollhouse — not *toys*, but rather masterful miniaturizations of the very pieces that adorned the homes of the past and add a festive glow to today's Christmas rooms.

Among the skilled craftspeople who recreate accessories from the past for small-scale vintage or contemporary Christmas settings is Richmond, Virginia, artist Ron Benson, who believes that his professional experience buying, selling and authenticating real antiques complements his hands-on studio efforts to reproduce them as porcelain miniatures. "I have the advantage of nearly 25 years in the antiques trade, working with the genuine artifacts," Ron explains. "I know how to direct my miniatures research. Instead of finding a 'cute' item, I look for specific examples of what I know was popular art in the period. I seek out details that separate the good from the very best, and sometimes I reproduce the popular version of an object rather than a finer but less commercially successful one. I want dollhouses to contain porcelains that were familiar to the average person, not esoteric museum pieces alien to middle-class settings."

By the afternoon of Christmas Day, when giftwrap, ribbons and relatives fill every corner of the house, the sink is piled with dishes and the fridge is packed with two weeks worth of leftover turkey and stuffing, family pets invariably go crazy. Mr. Calm, that supremely dignified feline, claws his way to the top of the tree and swallows the tinsel. Hamlet, normally a sad-eyed melancholic beagle, rampages through wrappings, overturns the punch bowl and makes off with Uncle Joe's expensive new tie. Upstate New York miniaturist Gail Morey is expert in the whys and wherefores of canine party syndrome, and every one of her realistic 1in (3cm), ½in (1cm) and ¼in (.65cm) dogs — she makes 70 breeds, each meticulously hand-carved from Sculpey® and painted by the artist — is ready and willing to add its cheery bit to holiday chaos in miniature. Gail also designs and furnishes whimsical room boxes "peopled" by her lovable canines; her prize-winning "I Believe in Santa-Paws" setting is described and pictured in our "More Animal Santas" chapter.

For believers in Santa Claus, as well as Santa-Paws, dollhouse doll artists provide a bountiful harvest of stunning examples, each colored by the individual thrust of its doll maker creator. The list of artists whose work includes Santa reads like a "Who's Who" of miniature doll making. Everyone seems to have attempted at least one Father Christmas. Thus, Janice Crawley, whose 6in (15cm) Jolly Santa poses beside the author's Victorian Toy Shop project — a well-sanded cigar box with lid converted to shelving and "drawers" in imitation of the 19th-century German toys we all covet but cannot afford.

Santa dolls appear on the show tables of Joan Benzell, Janna Joseph, Sheila Kwartler, Alaska-based Dorothy Hoskins and others. Dorothy Hoskins' "We Two - Miniatures" studio is best known for its extraordinary renderings of native Americans, but at the edge of the polar ice cap, Eskimo boys and girls and Father Christmas are surely neighbors. "The two subjects intermesh when you're up here in Fairbanks," Dorothy told us with a smile. "And when I put those darling children into a vignette with Santa, magic happens."

Dollhouse-scale Santas with a difference are made in the California studio of artist Helen Hartzell, whose doll-making career was launched in the mid 1980s and who found her focus in 1987 when she discovered the miniatures world. "I was crafting 16in (41cm) figures at the time and subscribed to a miniatures magazine with the idea that accessories described and advertised there might help complete my Santa groups," Helen explained. "Then I tried crafting a Santa in 1in (3cm) = 1ft (31cm) and fell head-over-heels in love with the scale. There's something really wonderful about being able to hold the entire figure in your hand."

For Helen, who began professionally as a florist and still keeps a greenhouse filled with 500 lovingly-cultivated orchids, Santa is an outdoor personality. "It's wrong, I feel, to put him inside houses. He wears warm outdoor clothing, is ruddy and windblown and comes from the forest and shadowy woods. I prepare bases and surrounds for my figures that include natural materials, particularly tree bark. I try to emphasize Santa's interrelationship with nature and the outside world." It is hardly surprising, considering her orientation, that Helen Hartzell's work includes Norwegian Yule Men, Wizards of The Woods, tiny elves and fairies 1in (3cm) high who often perch on Santa's shoulder or peek over his hat brim.

Indoor Santas are great too, according to Ohio artist Mary Hoot, best known for her extraordinarily lifelike dollhouse pets and woodland animals crafted from painted fabric. Mary has made a wide range of Santas down the years. "In fact, the second doll I ever made — at age six! — was a Santa Claus," the artist said with a grin. It was made from an old sock and had a very limited wardrobe. It wore a blue-and-white-striped nightgown, a cap and slippers!"

Mary, who claims she "was born with a paintbrush in her hand," prefers to work with a dimensional surface rather than simulate one on paper or canvas. Her dolls and painted fabric animals débuted on show tables in 1973 and were originally far larger than the miniature work she concentrates on today. The techniques used were the same, however, and the artist's "Saint Nicholas inspired by Grandma's cookie cutter," first designed as a 10in (25cm) tall flat-bottomed, cone-shaped Christmas Man is now offered as a charming 4in to 5in (10cm to 13cm) dollhouse piece. Mary Hoot loves to experiment with different techniques and has crafted polyform Santas and sculpted clay Santas with posable wire armature skeletons. "I'll do more with clay when I have time," she said, "but for now I'm concentrating on painted cloth figures and animals."

Outstanding in this brilliant company of dollhouse Santa craftspeople are the creations of Sylvia Lyons, the husband/wife team of Mary Penet and Phil LaVigne and Doreen Sinnett.

Sylvia Lyons' gorgeously costumed, fully-jointed Santas are dramatic works of art electric with theatrical energy, understandably so, since this California artist is also a dancer, with experience in staging, choreography and ballet. Sylvia first began designing dollhouse size dolls because she was disgusted with the awkward, rheumatic-jointed minikins available in the 1970s to populate dollhouses she crafted for various charities. "Have you ever propped a doll in a dollhouse, only to have the body look like someone had stuffed a coat hanger inside the shoulders so the head and neck disappear into the collar, turtle fashion?" she asked. "And have you noticed how, when some dolls sit on dollhouse chairs, their legs stick straight out and their arms hang stiffly at their sides? I'm a person and I have joints," Sylvia reasoned. "Little people need joints too." So she set about engineering dollhouse size dolls with the flex-

ibility of real live humans and after years of experimenting, developed the marvelous jointed porcelain figures for which she is known today.

Each Sylvia Lyons doll has real working joints and is strung with elastic. Costumes, for Santas as well as for hundreds of other doll subjects, are hand-sewn by the artist, whose studio cupboards overflow with laces, silks, organzas, trims, buttons and other fabric treasures garnered over the years. Sylvia is as meticulous in her research and costume design as she is in her effort to make her dolls more and more "alive," and the next step, having at last engineered a satisfactory, completely posable doll body, is to give her figures the capability to use their elegant joints. In the works are plans for motorized mini humans that walk in addition to sitting and standing in a convincingly natural manner.

Very different from Sylvia's posable Santas are the eerily lifelike 1in (3cm)-scale Christmas Men sculpted by Mary Penet and Phil LaVigne of Ann Arbor, Michigan. Dollhouse size dolls from this talented couple's studio range from absolute realism (flower sellers, mothers trimming piecrusts, everyday men and women from the 1930s and 1940s engaged in everyday activities), to utter fantasy (wizards, genies, "Uncle Bill Fishing," where the rowboat, Uncle Bill, hook, line and sinker are inside a goldfish bowl!).

Santa Claus is the fantasy figure Mary loves best. "When I sculpt Santas, I don't base my work on historical data," she said earnestly. "Any child knows exactly what Santa looks like. So when I turn to that subject, I draw on the magical feeling I used to have as a child (and still do!) every Christmas Eve. I know Santa has a bag of dreams to fulfill every wish. He has pockets filled with dreams I haven't even dreamed yet. His eyes glow with love and care for each of the world's good creatures — and for me. His smile tells each one of us how special we are. His clothes, lined with soft fur, trimmed with gold beads and tinkling bells, echo the fun he has bringing cheer to our humdrum lives. That's how I make my Santas," Mary concluded. "I've 'seen' him many times. Each Santa I sculpt has a life all his own; he is a refiltering of childhood dreams and fantasies."

Fantasy plays no part in the technical side of Penet/LaVigne Santa sculpting. Mary majored in art and theatre design at college, has sold her hand-made quilts and wall hangings through galleries and craft fairs and has created miniatures professionally since 1972. Phil is a brilliant painter (and a Michigan policeman!) whose delicate brushstrokes provide the glowing complexions and "living features" of PM Studio dolls. Mary rough molds, then fine carves her dolls from Super Sculpey® before passing them to Phil for painting. He applies a flat enamel primer followed by three layers of carefully blended airbrushed acrylic flesh tone overpainted with ex-

A 1987 French Père Noël for the dollhouse by Ann Arbor, Michigan master miniaturists Mary Penet and Phil LaVigne. Père Noël wears traditional Gallic robes with the classic grape basket strapped to his back and loaded with toys "pour les gentils petits enfants..." *Photograph by Patrick Müller. Courtesy of Poupée Tendresse, Paris, France.*

ABOVE RIGHT: A hybrid Father Christmas can be good art! Penet/LaVigne blended several traditions to come up with a whimsical Victorian with ruddy Coca-Cola® Santa cheeks and girth and a long-stemmed New Amsterdam Dutch pipe. *Photograph courtesy of Mary Penet and Phil LaVigne.*

"I sit in front of the fireplace on Christmas Eve," quips Ann Arbor, Michigan, artist Mary Penet, "and whatever comes down the chimney, I translate into art." *Ergo* this fantasy Bishop Saint Nick with his miter, crook and unorthodox patchwork sack crammed with goodies for the children. *Photograph courtesy of Mary Penet and Phil LaVigne.*

quisitely expressive features. Mary wigs and costumes the figures which, when completed, are magnificent freestanding Santas with faces and costumes ranging from pure fairytale to Victorian to Coca-Cola® 1940s. Each and every one began as a lump of clay in the artist's hand and a vision of magic in the artist's imagination.

Few miniature doll makers have demonstrated the professional-quality versatility that is the hallmark of California artist Doreen Sinnett. Doreen has designed rug kits, cast mini bricks, created do-it-yourself doll kits from cloth, porcelain and clothespins. She has also created brilliant one-of-a-kind Father Christmas dolls that star in fabulous seasonal vignettes across our country and abroad. Two of Doreen's dolls, now in Ingeborg Riesser's famous collection in Paris, France, are illustrated here — one a 1985 Sleeping Santa, exhausted by pre-holiday workshop pressures, the other a delightful Jolly Santa that photographer Patrick Müller "snapped" en route down a lucky French chimney.

Unlike most dollhouse Santas meant for inclusion in existing settings, the Christmas people in Lauren's Santa's Workshop at Angels Attic Miniature Museum are components in a larger design. The "Workshop," on view in the museum's Santa Monica, California, galleries from Thanksgiving through mid January each year, was begun in late 1976 and took almost two years to complete. It is three stories high, 6½ft (2m, 15cm) long and consists of four interlocking sections.

The artist behind this delightful fantasy is Bill Pickerill, whose expertise as a miniatures craftsperson derives from a long career as a model maker for Hollywood film studios. Bill designed and constructed the shell for this elaborate Christmas dollhouse. He also hand shaped the tiles for kitchen and courtyard, designed the complex lighting system, laid all hardwood floors, built the "built-ins" and developed the special textured material used for exterior surfacing. Elves are by well-known California doll maker Cynthia Baron; unfortunately, the artist who crafted the delightful Santa and Mrs. Claus is not known. Santa's Workshop was purchased for Angels Attic in 1985 as a gift in memory of Museum Founder Jackie McMahon's older granddaughter, Lauren Kay McLaughlin, who was killed in a tragic automobile accident at age 19. "Lauren always loved Christmas," Assistant Museum Director Eleanor LaVove said simply.

A very different Christmas experience, miniaturized, awaits the visitor to John Blauer's Maynard Manor, the gargantuan, 42-room dollhouse complex that houses the internationally-acclaimed collection at San Francisco's Miniature Mart. Santa's presence is felt but not seen in the Manor's lavish Entrance Hall, Toy Room and Christmas Room, each filled with gorgeous 1in (3cm) scale artwork by name artists (including John and Ellen Blauer) and work by master craftspeople from the past whose names are unknown.

John Blauer must have miniatures in his blood! When his grandmother fled her home during the 1906 San Francisco earthquake, the object she slipped into her purse and preserved was a tiny porcelain tea set. John's father, a master jeweler at Shreve and Company for 50 years, taught his son to appreciate the beauty which a trained hand can create within a small compass.

Throughout his California boyhood, John collected small art objects and assembled dioramas depicting battle scenes and farmyard settings. A gift box filled with Chinese furniture inspired his first miniature room, but it was the sight of the Thorne Rooms at the 1939 World's Fair that really triggered his enthusiasm for room box settings. He went home and crafted seven, filling them with his own artwork and with pieces from his already-burgeoning collection. When he asked local cabinetmakers to build a container to house his miniature rooms, however, he hit a snag. "I went to five cabinetmakers and asked them to construct Maynard Manor to my specifications. They all told me that if this was to be a dollhouse, it was much too big." When John contacted a sixth cabinetmaker, he changed his approach. "I said I wanted three bookcases with glass doors. The man questioned the dimensions of the center section (the 41in [1m, 5cm]-high Entrance Hall), and I told him that was storage space for maps and charts. Luckily, he went along with that. After I got the basic structure, I started to add architectural enhancements myself. It's a project that's been in progress for over 30 years."

Father Christmas works the same powerful magic in the dollhouse as he does in the big houses we really live in. And like the real Santa Claus who infuses warmth and love into the winter season each December, dollhouse Santas work their special magic, seen or unseen. In the 1920s, Sir Nevile Wilkinson created Titania's Palace, one of the century's most remarkable dollhouses. In the Hall of The Fairy Kiss, the room in which Sir Nevile placed the most wonderful of his fairytale treasures, stands an exquisite sleigh which, we are told, is made available at Christmas time to Santa Claus. The sleigh, crafted from pure gold and surrounded by a rail of silver inset with agates, may be less practical than the swell-body Albany cutter suggested as the ideal vehicle for his purpose by expert Carol Hardy, but, Carol agrees, it is an appropriately "magic" tribute to one of the world's most magical personalities.

A 20th-century American Santa Claus contemplates a 20th-century cloth doll in the Raggedy Ann and Andy tradition. In photographs, Mary and Phil's dolls are often mistaken for gorgeously clothed real live actors. *Photograph courtesy of Mary Penet and Phil LaVigne.*

An apple shared between friends! Mary Penet designed and sculpted this marvelous group. Her talented husband, Phil LaVigne, completed the painting that brings it to life. *Photograph courtesy of Mary Penet and Phil LaVigne.*

California dollhouse doll artist Doreen Sinnett poses in her porcelain pouring room. Shelves are loaded with molds Doreen uses to create her famous mini people. *Photograph by Diana West. Courtesy of Doreen Sinnett.*

A delectable 1989 Santa setting from Inge Riesser's Paris collection. Santa is by California artist Doreen Sinnett; the lucky home about to receive its annual holiday visit is from the British studio of Bryan and Judith Poole. Toys are by British, French and American contemporary miniatures artists. *Photograph by Patrick Müller. Courtesy of Poupée Tendresse, Paris, France.*

BELOW LEFT: Santa's elves work overtime during the pre-holiday rush each year. The 1in (3cm) = 12in (31cm) workshop/dollhouse at Angels Attic is loaded with finished work ready for distribution to good dollhouse boys and girls worldwide! *Photograph courtesy of Angels Attic, Santa Monica, California.*

Santa, Mrs. Santa and a bevy of elves from the studio of Cynthia Baron bustle about their chores inside Santa's 6½ft (2m, 15cm) long, 5½ft (1m, 76cm) high workshop, a structure that was two years a-building. *Photograph courtesy of Angels Attic, Santa Monica, California.*

Ready and waiting for Santa's nocturnal visit, the famous Entrance Hall of John Blauer's Maynard Manor boasts a wonderful Christmas tree decorated with over 80 ornaments, tiny toys and bisque dolls. Among the 50 individually-wrapped packages that surround the tree, three have been unwrapped to reveal a tiny coronation coach, a jack-in-the-box and assorted Christmas candies. *Photograph courtesy of The Miniature Mart, San Francisco, California.*

Miniature masterpieces of toy and doll art fill the fabulous toy room within the Maynard Manor complex. Tiny treasures include dolls, dollhouses, Vienna bronze Beatrix Potter animals, three of Elaine Cannon's fully-costumed grain-of-wheat dolls, tiny figures by Cynthia Baron, picture blocks and a puppet theatre by Hemy Eppich. *Photograph courtesy of The Miniature Mart, San Francisco, California.*

The fabulous Christmas Room in Maynard Manor may be where Santa stores his truly priceless mini treasures. Included among the playthings that fill this setting are numerous tiny dolls by Irma Park, Jean Wilson, Martha Farnsworth and Joyce Lynch. *Photograph courtesy of The Miniature Mart, San Francisco, California.*

Santa Bears

Rare and unusual, this circa 1909 Santa Bear is 10½in (27cm) tall with jointed limbs and felt pads. Fur is deep blue; painted celluloid head with molded hat. *From the collection of Susan Brown Nicholson.*

Legend recounts how Teddy Roosevelt went a'hunting, spared a cub, and the teddy bear was born. So, in fact, was the Santa Bear, whose history is as venerable as that of the rest of his hump-backed, long-muzzled, straw-stuffed ancestral kith and kin!

Most early Santa Bear survivors are nursery dressed, makeshift and adorable. Consider the pair shown here, neither of which began life as a Christmas Bear. Some thoughtful Nanny or gifted nursery denizen stitched and crafted the costumes that blended with Teddy's mystique and stuck. A commercial piece is the circa 1909 10½in (27cm) Santa Bear (*Cf.* illustration) from the Illinois collection of Susan Brown Nicholson. The bear has jointed limbs and felt pads, with deep blue fur, painted celluloid (human) head and molded hat that once matched the blue fur body. The figure is too charming to reflect the gloomy Knecht Ruprecht tradition, and his unknown maker's intention may forever remain a mystery.

If commercially-manufactured Santa Bears were uncommon early in the century, that is hardly the case today. With bear collecting a top-priority collector focus, big and small studios as well as large-scale commercial efforts vie to produce stunning, often droll, teddies that echo every aspect of day-to-day experience in the 1990s. Thus, the North American Bear Company has released a series of beary charming parodies of historic and topical personali-ties, from Clawed Monet (a VanderBear painter resident at Gibearny!), to Marlon Bearando dressed as a motorcyclist, and Red Octobear, who wears a Soviet naval kit. North American has a Bearlock Holmes, Bearilyn Monroe, Bearb Ruth and Albeart Einstein. Of course, Saint Nicholas appears among this diverse and fuzzy company, with a Victorian St. Nick issued in 1989 and a 1990 "Twas The Night Bearfore Xmas" V.I.B. (Very Important Bear) dressed in drop seat longjohns with "fur"-trimmed hat and slippers. North American's popular Muffy Bear also took a 1990 holiday bow, costumed as "Muffy Fir Tree," 7in (18cm) tall, holding "a partridge in a bear tree."

From commercial bears to artist bears, from Steiff to Dee Hockenberry's 13in (33cm) 1990 Saint Nicholas Bear, top-quality Santa Bears are proliferating almost as fast as top-quality artist *doll* Santas. And like all good art, each bear reflects the personality and artistic thrust of the studio that produced it.

Donna Bobby of Virginia Beach, Virginia, explained how a lifelong love of art, teddies and Christmas fused in the mid 1980s, when she went public as a teddy bear artist. Her success was immediate and her "Forest Glen Studio" has released dozens of bears, including several delightful Santas inspired by love and given stylistic direction by Donna's long-time antique German and American Santa collection. In 1989, she made a Patriotic Santa Bear and, for the 1990 Teddy Bear Convention and Show in Baltimore, where the theme was "Teddy Bears on

Broadway," she created a darling 18in (46cm) "Miracle on 34th Street Bear."

Everyone whose teddy bear art includes Santa Bears has a very personal tale to explain his or her focus. And every year the list of Santa Bear artists grows longer, with stunning work produced since the mid 1980s by Penny Noble, Lori Gardiner, Steve Shutt, Althea Leistikow, Carol Loucks, Beverly Matteson Port, Linda Spiegel, Karen Haskell, Gary Nett, Heather Smith (Canadian), Ballard Baines and many, many more. The point of entry into teddy bear-dom for each of these many gifted artists is always fascinating and is occasionally fraught with real trauma.

Sue Ellen Foskey's story may strike a familiar chord for many artists and collectors. "My mother saw all stuffed toys as unhygienic dustcatchers," Sue said with a rueful smile. "So my only childhood teddy bear was given to the trashman when I was four years old. I was out in the yard one morning," Sue recounted, "when the garbage man came to collect the trash. Seeing Teddy in the pile, he strapped it to the side of the truck, probably to take home to his own children. I happened to spot Teddy and ran after the truck crying 'Teddy! Come back!' When my mother saw me running down the street, she also took off after the truck. She managed to catch the driver, and I won round one. But when I wasn't looking, Teddy was thrown away a second time, never to be seen again. I don't remember what Teddy looked like; I don't even have a photograph."

Teddy was destined to climb back into Sue's world. Today, years later, Sue and her husband, Randall, happily collect antique teddy bear "dustcatchers" and, for the past seven/eight years, have designed and crafted some of the best artist bears of our times, among them the Santa Bears pictured here.

A number of the teddy bear artists whose work we illustrate — among them Lori Gardiner, Beverly and Kimberlee Port, Deanna Brittsan and others — have been featured repeatedly in books and magazines, and their stories are known to collectors. Less familiar, perhaps, is the tale behind the crocheted mini teddies made by New Hampshire artist Maggie Anderson, whose first Santa Bear was produced a mere four years ago.

Maggie Anderson first picked up a crochet hook in the late 1970s, when a pattern she had purchased turned out to be for a crocheted rather than a knitted garment. Crocheting was fun, but she was soon bored by conventional projects. "The way I look at it," Maggie told us, "anyone who can wrap the telephone cord around her finger can crochet anything if she has access to the right pattern." Maggie's patterns moved quickly from commercial to personally designed. Soon, she began experimenting with 3-D crocheted dolls, toys and stuffed animals, and

loves to recount the amusing challenge that was her first 1in (3cm) scale teddy bear.

"A member of our local doll club saw one of my 12in (31cm) crocheted bears and asked me to make one like it, but smaller, for her dollhouse. I went home and crocheted a bear about 4in (10cm) tall, only to learn that she wanted teddy for her *dollhouse nursery cupboard*, so 4in was way too big. I bought some Knit-Cro-Sheen® and made a 2in (5cm) bear which the lady said was 'sweet but still a little bit too large.' I thought, 'What does she want from me? Has she any idea how hard it was making that 2in bear? Does she know how difficult it will be just to find suitable yarn for a smaller bear?' I went home, shoved all my yarn aside, searched through my crochet hooks for the smallest one (Size 13) and crocheted a bear ¾in (2cm) tall out of sewing thread. I personally drove him to her house and she screamed 'That's it!' And I've been making tinies ever since."

Teddy #1 was followed by the merry menagerie of irrepressible mini bears for which this I.G.M.A. Fellow is known today. Maggie makes Happy New Year and Birthday Bears, Edwardian Bears, Smokeys, Pirates, Indians, Wee Scots, Paddingtons, Winnie-the-Poohs, roller-skating bears and bear fishermen. Her "tinies," which average 1¼in (3cm) tall, include mermaid bears (with shimmering green tails, of course), chef bears, a limited edition Miss LiBearty, and the Santa Claus Bears shown here. Maggie's first crocheted mini Santa Bear, made in 1989, had a detachable beard. "He was a 'phoney,'" the artist told us. "I deplore the commercialism of modern Christmas, and that bear was my statement of defiance!" Soon, however, Maggie's attitude softened, and recent Santa Bear "tinies" are delightful in Victorian robes, "real" whiskers, classic two-piece Coca-Cola® Santa suits and packing full toy sacks. Some of her holiday bears sport dozens of in-scale accessories, sit on mini sleighs crafted by husband Hank Anderson, even carry crocheted Christmas stockings in lieu of the traditional pack. "I make bears because I love to make bears," this delightful craftswoman says with a smile. "And Santa has definitely taken an upfront position among my favorite subjects."

The same can be said for all teddy bear artists who have included Father Christmas among their offerings in recent years — big character bears by Nancy Crowe of Lansing, Michigan, hilarious comic bears like Californians Jodi and Richard Creager's 16in (40cm) Polar Bear Santa, now part of the permanent collection of Ingeborg Riesser of Paris, France, dainty minis like Elaine Fujita-Gamble's "Cubby Christmas" and Seattle artist Janie Comito's "bears in all sizes." All this is the beginning, not the end of the subject! Collectors who think *bears* are the only anthropomorphic interpretations of everybody's favorite Christmas Man are advised to turn the page and greet a veritable zoo-full of More Animal Santas!

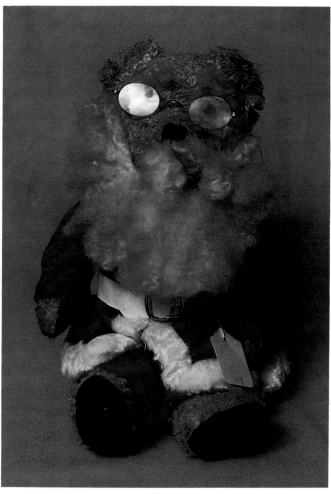

A 16in (41cm) fully-articulated antique teddy sports a home-crafted red velvet Santa suit and real spectacles! Bear is yellow plush with glass eyes and velvet paws. *Photograph courtesy of Swanson's Auctions, Mountain Center, California.*

ABOVE LEFT: A much-loved gold mohair antique teddy with jointed arms and legs, glass eyes, satin pads and floss-stitched smile sits tall in his early-20th-century two-piece Santa suit. Bear is 17in (43cm). *Photograph courtesy of Swanson's Auctions, Mountain Center, California.*

North American Bear Company's 1990 V.I.B. 'Twas The Night Before Xmas Santa Bear. He wears flap-back longjohns with "fur-trimmed" hat and slippers and stands a mighty 20in (51cm) tall. *Photograph courtesy of The North American Bear Company, Chicago, Illinois.*

Dee Hockenberry's 13in (33cm) 1990 Saint Nicholas Bear. Pale cinnamon mohair, fully jointed with felt pads, black glass shoebutton eyes, embroidered nose, mouth and claws. He wears a velvet robe and cap with fox-colored fur trim. Gold cord sash with brass French horn. *Photograph courtesy of Dee Hockenberry.*

ABOVE RIGHT: Donna Bobby's traditional white (polar bear?) Santa Bear shares a hardwood sleigh with a mass of Christmas goodies, to gladden the hearts and fill the tummies of cubs worldwide! *Photograph by Mat Bobby. Courtesy of Donna Bobby.*

From Donna Bobby's Virginia studio comes this "Father Forest," made especially for the *Santa Dolls* book. The gentleman is 23in (58cm) tall and made of distressed "vanilla" mohair. Coat is wine-colored nubby chenille trimmed with synthetic fur from Germany. The pouch is stuffed with natural treasures from the deep, deep woods. *Photograph by Jim Chalkley. Courtesy of Donna Bobby.*

12in (31cm) antique reproduction Teddy Bear Santa made of mohair distressed by hand, straw stuffed, with real old-fashioned leather shoebutton eyes. Artist Sue Foskey made the coat of antique red wool trimmed with genuine mink. *Photograph by Randall S. Foskey. Courtesy of The Nostalgic Bear Company.*

ABOVE LEFT: Joan Woessner's 1990 Victorian Father Christmas Bear complete with bear-on-all-fours reindeer substitute to help lug the goodies. Father Christmas is 17in (43cm) tall and wears burgundy velvet trimmed with real mink. Joan says it took her a full year to collect the toys and trimmings for this charming group. *Photograph courtesy of Joan and Mike Woessner, Bear Elegance.*

Sue Foskey's 12in (31cm) antique reproduction bear, carrying more traditional goodies, wears a coat trimmed with white rabbit fur. *Photograph by Randall S. Foskey. Courtesy of The Nostalgic Bear Company.*

Deanna Brittsan's Victorian Santa and Christmas Gnome seated on a sleigh crafted by Deanna's husband. The distressed mohair 18in (46cm) Santa wears a 1914 crazy quilt trimmed with alpaca, belted with a gold chain from which hang a horn and a toy drum. *Photograph courtesy of Deanna Brittsan.*

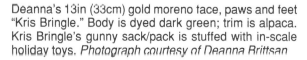

Deanna's 13in (33cm) gold moreno face, paws and feet "Kris Bringle." Body is dyed dark green; trim is alpaca. Kris Bringle's gunny sack/pack is stuffed with in-scale holiday toys. *Photograph courtesy of Deanna Brittsan.*

A special order from a California collector inspired Maggie Anderson's extraordinary 1½in (4cm) Santa Bear with sleigh and toys. All the goodies are hand-crafted by name miniatures artists, with wooden objects and the sleigh from the studio of Maggie's gifted husband, Hank Anderson. *Photograph by Peter Groesbeck. Courtesy of Maggie Anderson.*

A playful bit of fist-shaking by New Hampshire bear artist Maggie Anderson who deplores the commercialization of Christmas in the 1990s. This Santa is a "phoney." He looks like the real McCoy, right? *Photograph by Peter Groesbeck. Courtesy of Maggie Anderson.*

Wrong!! Both the costume *and the beard* come off!! An amazing accomplishment by this gifted needle artist since, from the soles of Santa's tiny feet to the peak of his hood, he measures a scant 1½in (4cm). *Photograph by Peter Groesbeck. Courtesy of Maggie Anderson.*

Kimberlee Port's 4in (10cm) "Christopher Christmas" with miniature bears 1in to 2in (3cm to 5cm) tall. All are crafted from a vintage short plush no longer obtainable; all are fully jointed — even the head on the 1in (3cm) bear! *Photograph by Norm Garner 1990. Courtesy of Kimberlee Port Bears.*

ABOVE RIGHT: A group of fabulous Christmas bears by Kimberlee Port. Included are her sensational "Teddy, Teddy Tree" made of green mohair, with battery-operated blinking lights and topped with a fully-jointed 1¼in (3cm) "Teddy Star;" 8in (20cm) fully-jointed Santa Bear; Ted. E. Bear posed with sled, and "Little Gold," 2½in (6cm) small, holding a wreath in his felt pawpads. *Photograph by Norm Garner 1990. Courtesy of Kimberlee Port Bears.*

A family group by Beverly and Kimberlee Port, features Beverly's 6in (15cm) Father Christmas and assorted bears by daughter Kimberlee. Bears range from ¾in (2cm) to 2½in (4cm) "Mr. Christmas Bear." *Photograph courtesy of Kimberlee Port Bears.*

Lori Gardiner's Father Christmas bear, 16in (41cm) tall, is made of green/gold mohair and wears a sage green velvet robe with gold braid trim and gold brocade detailing. His sack conceals a touch-activated music box. "I looked all over to find this color mohair and velvet, the color real Victorian Santas often wore," Lori told us. *Photograph courtesy of Lori Gardiner, Echoes of the Past.*

BELOW LEFT: Elaine Fujita-Gamble's 1990 fully-jointed Cubby Christmas stands a diminutive 2¾in (7cm) tall. Cubby wears a red velvet jacket and hood, green velvet mittens and pants and black boots. "Frosty" is papier-mâché and "Bear Pal" is a fully-jointed mini cub wrapped around with a cozy flannel muffler. *Photograph courtesy of George Comito.*

Outstanding miniature Father Christmas mohair bear by Washington state artist Elaine Fujita-Gamble. Bear measures 4in (10cm), is dressed in red wool and loaded with toys! *Photograph courtesy of George Comito.*

Another bear pair from Janie's Seattle studio, this time an 8½in (22cm) Bear Nicholas with a 4in (10cm) teddy. Both are mohair and jointed. *Photograph courtesy of Janie Comito.*

Janie Comito's 1990 4in (10cm) Bear Nicholas gives a boost up to Mini Nick, 1½in (4cm). Bears are fully jointed and wear real leather boots. *Photograph courtesy of Janie Comito.*

Perhaps the ultimate in mini Santa Bear-dom, Janie Comito's 3in (8cm) Bear Nicholas sits proudly in a handmade wooden sleigh pulled by (what else!) a polar bear! *Photograph courtesy of Janie Comito.*

Nancy Crowe's old-fashioned 13in (33cm) Father Christmas bear made of wavy cream mohair. His handmade basket overflows with holiday greenery, and he wears a finely detailed coat of claret wool with alpaca lining and designer trim. Photograph by Kim Kauffman Photography, Inc. Courtesy of Nancy Crowe.

Nancy Crowe's 15in (38cm) Saint Nicholas sports an elegant red velveteen cloak lined with gilded, bird-festooned cotton and trimmed with German braid. Toy sack and evergreen crown tipped at a jaunty angle lend zest and pizzaz to this jolly figure. *Photograph by Kim Kauffman Photography, Inc. Courtesy of Nancy Crowe.*

Florida artist Carol Stewart turned the Santa Bear idea around to produce a *real* Santa Claus loaded with *real* holiday collector bears! Santa is 7in (18cm) tall; the smallest bear measures ¾in (2cm). *Photograph courtesy of Carol Stewart, Custom Teddy Bears.*

A 16in (40cm) 1990 Polar Bear Santa Claus by Jodi and Richard Creager, poses with a girl bear by Carol-Lynn Rössel Waugh and 1990 bears by Steiff and Odette Conley. *Photograph by Patrick Müller. Courtesy of Poupée Tendresse, Paris, France.*

More Animal Santas

Two Father Christmas mice from Germany, costumed by different groups here in the United States. One Santa is timid and (forgive the pun) "mousy;" the other is royal and nearly overwhelmed by runaway whiskers. The larger mouse is 2in (7cm) tall. *Photograph by Peter Groesbeck.*

If you think Father Christmas teddies and Janice Crawley's one-of-a-kind animal Santas in cloth or porcelain complete the zoological side of Christmas dolldom, guess again! For there exists a fabulous substratum of artists and collectors in love with a vast population of animal people that echo one or another of several curious and venerable traditions.

Some animal dolls are merely dressed beasts, blessed with the paws and natural shape as well as the head peculiar to their species. Dolls of this sort echo the "hedgerow, farmyard and wainscot animals" immortalized by Beatrix Potter's turn-of-the-century tales and watercolors. They share a common heritage with American children's author Howard R. Garis's Uncle Wiggily Longears, Nurse Jane Fuzzy Wuzzy and Jackie and Peetie Bow Wow the puppy-dog boys; with de Brunhoff's Babar, with Anatole the Mouse, with Frances the Badger — in fact, with every first-rate childhood favorite in which creatures wear clothes and behave like humans, without breaking faith with their essentially animal natures.

A very different school of thought extends the fantasy to create drawings, dolls and collector figures that are human in every way except for their heads. Such "animal people" are directly descended from the enchanting, satirical 19th-century tradition established by Grandville and extended by Tenniel. The goat gentleman who shared the railway compartment with Alice in *Through the Looking-Glass* is a case in point. And locked forever into our collective

A pair of handmade British Christmas mice, 3in (8cm) tall. On the left, Saint Lucy, wearing her traditional crown of holiday candles; on the right, a beguiling lace-clad angel. *Photograph by Peter Groesbeck.*

Pennsylvania folk artist Judy Grocki, whose work is discussed in detail in the section of this book devoted to contemporary artists, crafted Santa and Mrs. Rabbit as well as Munchkin Claus. Figures are hand-sewn from cloth and jointed at hips and shoulders. *Photograph by Peter Groesbeck. Courtesy of Judy Grocki.*

New York State artist Gail Morey's dollhouse-scale room box titled "I Believe in Santa Paws" has been the hit of the show again and again. Note Father Dog's Santa suit half-hidden behind the wing chair. Mama Dog is decorating the tree with white doggie bones (of course!), and sleepy puppies play and dream of the magic to come on Christmas morning. *Photograph courtesy of Gail Morey.*

Artist Lulie Sabella at work in her Santa Monica, California, studio. *Photograph courtesy of Lulie Sabella.*

Three ½in to 1 ft (1 cm to 31cm) scale fantasy Santas by California artist Lulie Sabella. Lulie's elephant and polar bear with sacks are ready to start their annual round. Frog Santa, with his work apron and tools, has yet to complete the "preliminaries"... *Photograph by Peter Groesbeck. Courtesy of Lulie Sabella.*

The logo of this California studio, "It's a jungle in here!" aptly describes Lulie Sabella's fantasy animal kingdom. Here are two of the artist's ½in (1cm) scale tongue-in-cheek Santa Clauses, one a killer shark, the other a penguin. ("Hey! Wait a minute, Lulie! He's from the **south** *pole!*") *Photograph by Peter Groesbeck. Courtesy of Lulie Sabella.*

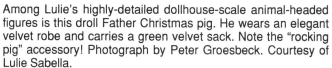

Among Lulie's highly-detailed dollhouse-scale animal-headed figures is this droll Father Christmas pig. He wears an elegant velvet robe and carries a green velvet sack. Note the "rocking pig" accessory! Photograph by Peter Groesbeck. Courtesy of Lulie Sabella.

ABOVE RIGHT: A reindeer Santa Claus from Lulie's Zoo wears antlers crafted from dental plastic by Hollywood friend Adam deFelice, who specializes in "creatures and model making" for the film industry. *Photograph by Peter Groesbeck. Courtesy of Lulie Sabella.*

A hippo-headed Father Christmas, one of the very few Santas Lulie Sabella has dressed in red. When she researched antique postcard Father Christmases, she told us, she was amazed how "un-red" their costumes were. In addition to the Shackman book, the sack contains a teddy bear by Frances Armstrong and a jointed peg doll by Eric Horne. *Photograph by Peter Groesbeck. Courtesy or Lulie Sabella.*

This Christmas walrus from Lulie's Zoo stands 6in (15cm) tall, its fierce tusks crafted from dental plastic by Hollywood model maker Adam deFelice. One wonders how youngsters "all snug in their beds" would react if *this* fellow emerged from the family chimney. *Photograph by Peter Groesbeck. Courtesy of Lulie Sabella.*

Like all of Lulie's 1in (3cm) scale animal-headed characters, this gorilla Father Christmas is designed to mingle with the human inhabitants of the dollhouse. His robe is trimmed with real Persian lamb. *Photograph by Peter Groesbeck. Courtesy of Lulie Sabella.*

Curtain call by Hollywood actress Lulie Sabella's dollhouse-size delightful (if surprising) Father Christmases. Taking an extra bow are her Reindeer Santa, Santa Hippo, "Russian" Gorilla Santa Claus, Pig Father Christmas and a very *toothsome* Walrus Claus! *Photograph by Peter Groesbeck. Courtesy of Lulie Sabella.*

Tyber Katz© 1991 limited edition "Santa Klaws" is 22in (56cm) tall and has a hefty middle 27in (69cm) around! He is free-standing with poseable arms and real horsehair whiskers. The toys, all handmade by the Tybers, are specially designed to delight "nursery kittens"! *Photograph courtesy of Tyber Katz©, Roseburg, Oregon.*

A purr-fectly marvelous Father Christmas made by Tyber Katz© as a 1987 limited edition of 50. The artists claim that "collectors could search the world and never again find a hand-carved, hand-painted wooden 'kat' with horsehair whiskers, dressed in a Victorian Santa suit!" Father Kristmas is 16in (41cm) tall and carries a bag filled with hand-carved toys — a sled, a pulltoy horse, a guitar and a tiny, hand-painted kitten doll with movable arms and legs. *Photograph courtesy of Tyber Katz©, Roseburg, Oregon.*

BELOW: A 1989 *Animal Christmas Party* by Wisconsin artist Karen Meer. Seated at a 3 ft (91cm) party table are six 15in to 17in (38cm to 43cm) animals and their host and hostess, Mr. and Mrs. Santa Claus. The elephant, zebra, pig, giraffe, lion, horse and Clauses are all handcrafted and handpainted and have embroidered features. *Photograph courtesy of Karen A. Meer. Oconomowoc, WI.*

memory are those two immortals, the frog and fish footmen from *Alice's Adventures in Wonderland*.

"...suddenly a footman in livery came running out of the wood — (she considered him to be a footman because he was in livery: otherwise, judging by his face alone, she would have called him a fish) — and rapped loudly at the door with his knuckles. It was opened by another footman in livery, with a round face and large eyes like a frog; and both footmen, Alice noticed, had powdered hair that curled all over their heads.

The Fish-Footman began by producing from under his arm a great letter, nearly as large as himself, and this he handed over to the other, saying in a solemn tone, 'For the Duchess. An invitation from the Queen to play croquet.' The Frog-Footman repeated, in the same solemn tone, only changing the order of the words a little, 'From the Queen. An invitation for the Duchess to play croquet.'

Then they both bowed low, and their curls got entangled together."

Animal Santas, like other animal dolls and storybook characters, may be dressed animals or animal-people, depending on the art orientation and purpose of their creators. The author's collection includes dressed Christmas mice hand-crafted in Germany and the United Kingdom. An adorable foursome — two Santas, a Saint Lucy and a Christmas angel — they are charming because each is 100% **MOUSE**, so much so that a previous German mouse was attacked, kidnapped and horribly mutilated by the family cat! One supposes the cat's intention was to rid the world of a freak, since the German mice, with their pipe cleaner legs and red bead noses, are "furred" with rabbit!

A good step up the sophistication ladder is the Judy Grocki trio pictured here — Mr. and Mrs. Santa Rabbit and Munchkin Claus who landed by default among our Christmas animals since neither Judy nor the author could establish to what genus Munchkins belong. Like Judy's people Santas discussed elsewhere, the Clauses and Munchkin are individually designed and hand-sewn by this Pennsylvania artist. Each cloth doll is jointed at shoulders and hips and, true to the folk art tradition Judy's work emulates, joints are simple, strong thread anchored with beads.

Very different are the Sculpey® dogs crafted by New York miniaturist Gail Morey. Gail, whose mischievous pedigreed puppies appear in our "Santa Claus in The Dollhouse" chapter, particularly enjoys designing whimsical room boxes inhabited by dogs engaged in amusing human interactions. Her "Harry The Hustler" room box is a luridly-lit barroom scene with a tense game of pool in progress. Bartender and players are large tough dogs. Again and again, Gail's canines provide gently-satirical visual commentary about the human condition. The artist's "Chicago Doggie Deli" was inspired by a photo in *People* magazine. In 1985, she crafted a delightful vignette titled "Whining and Dining," in which a dollhouse-scale gentleman and lady dog share cocktails *al fresco*. "Of course, a Christmas dog setting was irresistible," Gail told us, pointing to her blue ribbon 1989 "I Believe in Santa-Paws" vignette.

"I created 'I Believe in Santa-Paws' with the help of my dad who built the room box and did the electrical work," the artist explained. "I wanted the viewer to feel the anticipation and excitement in the air. On the radio in the dogs' living room, voices are barking 'Jingle Bells.' Papa puffs on his cigar and reads 'Twas The Night Before Christmas' to pups sitting on the hearth rug in ecstatic anticipation of Santa-Paws' arrival. Mama puts finishing touches to a tree lavishly decorated with lights, garlands, bows and porcelain bones. *Where is Santa-Paws*? Well, Papa Dog is Santa-Paws, of course," Gail said with a smile. "Hidden behind his chair is a Santa-Paws outfit complete with boots and a beard plus a shopping bag filled with Christmas toys."

Gail Morey left no bone unturned in her Santa-Paws room box design. Walls are hung with family pawtraits; holiday stockings tacked to the mantel overflow with rawhide bones and juicy doggie treats. "The puppies have set out a glass of milk and a tray loaded with cookie bones for Santa-Paws. Soon they will retire for the night and you know the rest of the story..."

Across the continent from Gail's Unadilla, New York studio, Pat and Peter Tyber of Roseburg, Oregon, craft cats as enthusiastically as Gail crafts dogs. But Tyber kats [sic.], unlike Gail Morey's realistic mini canines, are whimsical high art, debonnaire and comically elegant.

Tyber Katz© was born when wood sculptor Peter Tyber carved and his cat portrait specialist wife Pat painted a Cheshire Grinning Wooden Cat doll for a very special nephew's Christmas surprise in December 1983. This first effort at combining their professional tracks was so successful among friends and relatives, the couple went on to design several tentative limited editions. These were welcomed by doll and folk-art collectors as well as by feline fanciers and today, eight years down the road from what Pat over-critically designates "very crude beginnings," Tyber Katz are sold through exclusive shops and galleries from Nantucket, Massachusetts, to Fairbanks, Alaska, as well as by mailorder directly from the artists.

Peter carves each limited edition Tyber kat or kitten (head and paws) from pine or basswood; Pat hand-paints carved elements with intricate detail, using a special technique to paint the eyes which *appear* to be glass. Wooden parts are sprayed with a protective coating, then wired to a soft muslin body. Whiskers are individually-inserted horsehair. Dolls are costumed as types or individuals. The Tybers have created Puss N' Boots, Prairie Kats, Vintage Sleepers (with beds, patchwork quilts and lace-edged pillows) and Tyber kittens adorable in muslin nighties. Their 18in (46cm) Golfer Kat sports plus fours, a striped shirt, argyle vest and a bow tie. His posh suede bag is well-stocked with brass-and-hardwood clubs. And, in 1986, the couple designed Les Chats Tyber, a family of exclusive, kid-bodied French Fashion Kats, truly the ultimate statement on the subject of feline elegance.

What kind of world would it be without Christmas Kats! Peter and Pat have given time and talent to creating a limited edition Victorian Father and Mother Kristmas and a bevy of darling Tyber Elves in leather work smocks or starched white parlormaid aprons, all wearing curly-toed elf shoes. In the Fall of 1991, they released a contemporary Santa Kat, different in design and mood from the earlier Victorian kats, but equally charming and popular among collectors. Naturally, work in the Tybers' busy Oregon studio is closely supervised by three spoiled, very much alive Tyber cats — Gran, Pooker and K.C.

The Santa Kats and holiday canines crafted by the Tybers and Gail Morey are very different from Beatrix Potter-esque dressed animal dolls. In fact, they inch along the fantasy scale toward the bizarre world of Grandville and Tenniel, with its fabulous animal-headed population. *Within* that curious society, few American artists can match the zany, funny commentary on the human condition reflected in the dollhouse dolls of Los Angeles artist Lulie Sabella.

"There aren't many people out there doing what I do," declares Hollywood actress/doll artist Lulie Newcomb Sabella, and she is right. For Lulie's extraordinary animal-headed dolls have guest starred on popular television series like "Perfect Strangers" where her husband, actor Ernie Sabella, plays the shop owner/landlord. An early set of posable dolls she designed from Maurice Sendak's drawings for the Pacific Northwest Ballet in 1982/1983 appeared on camera in "The Nutcracker Ballet." Animal heads from Lulie's Zoo® studio took a bow in *Fright Night* (Part II) where Ernie played the psychologist and, at the time of our visit, they were scheduled for yet another silver screen appearance, in a Fall 1990 Warner Brothers comedy release.

The talented artist behind these definitely off-the-beaten-track art dolls considers herself first and foremost a sculptress. Seeds for the thrust of her present work were sown during a childhood lived on a farm outside Seattle where she was surrounded by real animals and lavished love on dozens of hard plastic and soft-stuffed animal toys that she invariably preferred to dolls and dollhouses. "I gained on-location knowledge of animals — their appearance, their psychologies, their sometimes embarrassing similarities to humans," she told us. "I attended 4-H

Fairs and put my sheep, chickens and ducks into competitions. I got lots of firsthand life study out of those guys!"

When Lulie was 12, her big Christmas gift was a kiln, still in use in her Santa Monica studio long years later. But early work fired in that kiln did not include animal heads. Instead, Lulie crafted portrait dolls for friends with whom she performed in high school theatricals. "They were closing night gifts," she said. "I'd sculpt a figure that looked just like my friend in the character she played in our school production. Everybody loved the dolls and I got a lot of excellent practice for the future."

By 1981, Lulie was studying acting in New York City. She was also taking sculpting classes and working during the day at a pottery shop and gallery called Earthworks. Just for fun, she sculpted several doll-scale animal heads. A friend suggested she add bodies and costumes, then try to market them as unusual dolls. The Earthworks owner displayed the finished pieces, which sold well, but when Lulie approached the larger marketplace, she encountered problems. "All my early animal heads were 10in (25cm) - 12in (31cm) art-size dolls with porcelain heads and soft bodies," she explained. "I'd show them to galleries and they'd call them craft pieces. I'd show them to craft shops and they'd tell me they were gallery pieces. It was really frustrating. Individual collectors loved my work but I couldn't sell it. By then, I wanted to expand and develop into a full-time studio business, and I finally realized that the dolls would have to be bigger or smaller to fit a specific market."

With "smaller" in mind, Lulie began to attend miniature shows and, one memorable day in 1989, she met and became fast friends with miniature book artist Carol Wenk at a show in San Mateo, California. It was Carol who provided the *open sesame* Lulie had been seeking for nearly eight years.

Carol Wenk introduced Lulie to artisans and dealers within the miniatures community, who told her about the National Association of Miniature Enthusiasts (N.A.M.E.) — "Of course, I joined right away!" — and the International Guild of Miniature Artisans (I.G.M.A.) — "I joined that too!" Lulie plunged into miniature dolldom and never once looked back. Only a year into her new career, beautifully costumed animal-headed people from her Santa Monica "zoo" were already mixing freely with human inhabitants in dollhouses and art display cabinets across the country.

As an art doll sculptress who is also a professional actress, Lulie Sabella has enjoyed her double-track career. She has been featured in films and, on television, she has appeared in *Working Girl, Newhart, Mr. Belvedere* and *Vietnam War Stories.* The "show biz" connection spills over into the art studio. Cindy Schumacher, a studio helper who does everything from pouring molds to sewing trims, is training to be a cinematographer. And Adam de Felice, a friend who does detail work for Lulie as his hectic schedule and her studio animals require, is involved full-time in "creature work and model-making" for the film industry. Adam sculpted the walrus tusks and reindeer antlers for two of Lulie's "Christmas Men," using dental plastic, a material from which he regularly fashions horror film vampire teeth!

Today, Lulie Sabella makes very few large dolls like the ones she first sold through Earthworks in New York. Current dolls are dollhouse size or smaller, with porcelain heads, hands and feet and completely posable wire armature bodies. Costumes are crafted from carefully selected vintage fabrics, vintage furs and vintage trims. "I love to use unusual materials that complement my figures," the artist said. "I've highlighted doll costumes with unique textured fabrics, buttons, laces and furs that run the gamut from fox and Persian lamb to real colob monkey fur, a straight coarse hair that was all the rage in the '20s."

The clutch of Father Christmases Lulie designed especially for the *Santa Dolls* book represents the artist's first venture into Christmas dolldom. Before heading for the studio, she researched the subject carefully, dipping deep into the world of antique Christmas postcards, holiday scraps and antique ceramic or pressed paper Belsnickles. What she discovered surprised her. "The colors I saw in the antique postcard books were all delightfully unred," she told us. "You had your traditional guys, of course, but my search suggested that Santa can wear just about anything in just about any color. The one restriction is that his costume is nearly always patterned after historic European peasant dress. So my walrus and his friends are dressed in old-world peasant type robes, and the big gorilla is, very specifically, a Russian-style peasant."

The worlds of human and animal dolls meet at last in the ultimate holiday fantasy, inside the studio of Wisconsin artist Karen A. Meer. There, since 1985, Karen has crafted cloth folk doll animals, children and Mr. and Mrs. Claus, as components in her increasingly-well-known Party Animal Celebrations.

This remarkable craftswoman was raised in an environment overflowing with art talent and art collections. Her mother is a professional watercolorist; her father a jeweler/woodcarver. Karen trained as a public school art teacher, then established her own stained glass studio business and continued to "play with all sorts of crafts just for fun." Cloth doll making was part of that fun, so when she attended a Country Peddler Show in Kentucky, she put horse heads on a selection of her 16in (41cm) cloth dolls and displayed them as a partying group titled "Kentucky Derby Party," all seated around a doll-size table. The setting was a smash hit, sold out in three days, and the artist has not stopped designing and crafting animal head parties and cloth boy, girl and Santa dolls since.

Today, Karen offers her dolls singly or as parties complete with in-scale furniture, dishes, balloons and confetti. There are birthday, Halloween, wedding, Easter and, of course, Christmas parties, the last presided over by an appropriately-clad Saint Nick — in old-fashioned robes for the "Victorian Christmas Party," in conventional red suit for the contemporary one. It is easy to understand why, on four separate occasions, Karen's "Party Animal Celebrations" have been front window displays at The Museum of American Folk Art in New York City.

The Christmas parties, large or small, include a 3ft (1m) vintage or contemporary Santa Claus, a table, chairs, holiday wreaths, tabletop tree and all the goodies that turn a *tea* into a *tea party*. Animal sizes average 16in (41cm), with inches added or subtracted as species require. Santa, like Karen's birthday party girl dolls, is cloth with a papier-mâché/wax overlay face. Animals are cloth — designed, stuffed, assembled and costumed by the artist and her busy studio assistants. Fine detailing, however, is always done by Karen herself, who stripes the tigers, spots the giraffes and embroiders elegant designs on collars, cuffs, aprons and doll blouses.

Finished pieces, be they individual dolls or complete party settings, travel far when they leave the artist's Wisconsin studio. In our own country, they can be found in shops and galleries from Nantucket to Houston, in the collections of doll lovers, senators and theatrical people. They are offered for sale in Tokyo and in Germany and have found their way into at least one royal collection. Karen Meer's Animal Christmas Parties have not chalked up as many air miles as that most frequent flyer, Santa Claus, but they carry the same holiday message wherever they go, a message of joy and love conveyed through the magic of dolls.

Selected Bibliography

Allen, Alistair and Hoverstadt, Joan. *The History of Printed Scraps*. London, New Cavendish Books, 1983.

Ancelet-Hustache, Jeanne. *St. Nicholas*. New York, The Macmillan Company, 1962.

Ayers, Dottie and Harrison, Donna. **Advertising Art of Steiff: Teddy Bears & Playthings**. Cumberland, MD, Hobby House Press, Inc., 1990.

Bahar, Ann. "Santas of Yesterday and Today," *Dolls Magazine*. New York, Collector Communications Corporation, December 1989.

Barenholtz, Bernard and McClintock, Inez. *American Antique Toys, 1830-1900*. New York, Harry N. Abrams, Inc., 1980.

Barnett, James H. *The American Christmas: A Study in National Culture*. New York, The Macmillan Company, 1954.

Bartholomew, Charles. *Mechanical Toys*. Secaucus, New Jersey, Chartwell, 1979.

Baum, Frank Joslyn and McFall, Russell P. *To Please A Child: A Biography of L. Frank Baum*. Chicago, Reilly & Lee Co., 1961.

Baum, L. Frank. *The Life and Adventures of Santa Claus* [1902]. Reprinted by Dover Publications, Inc. New York, 1976.

Brenner, Robert. *Christmas Past*. West Chester, PA, Schiffer Publishing Ltd., 1985.

Buday, George. *The History of The Christmas Card*. London, Spring Books, 1964.

Bullard, Helen. **Faith Wick: Doll Maker Extraordinaire**. Cumberland, MD, Hobby House Press, Inc., 1986.

Coffin, Tristram P. *The Book of Christmas Folklore*. New York, The Seabury Press, 1973.

Coleman, Dorothy S., Elizabeth A. and Evelyn J. *The Collector's Encyclopedia of Dolls*. London, Robert Hale & Company, 1968.

Conway, Shirley and Wilson, Jean. *100 Years of Steiff*. Berlin, Ohio, Berlin Printing, 1980.

Ebon, Martin. *Saint Nicholas: Life and Legend*. New York, Harper & Row, Publishers, 1975.

Fawcett, Clara Hallard. *Collector's Guide to Antique Paper Dolls*, [1951]. Reprinted by Dover Publications, Inc., New York, 1989.

Foley, Dan. *Toys Through The Ages*. Philadelphia, Chilton Books, 1962.

Foulke, Jan. **8th Blue Book: Dolls and Values**®. Cumberland, MD, Hobby House Press, Inc., 1987.

Foulke, Jan. **9th Blue Book: Dolls and Values**®. Cumberland, MD, Hobby House Press, Inc., 1989.

Grender, Iris. *An Old-Fashioned Christmas*. London, Hutchinson of London, 1979.

Hart, C., Grossman, J., and Dunhill, P. *A Victorian Scrapbook*. New York, Workman Publishing Company, Inc., 1989.

Hart, C., Grossman, J., and Dunhill, P. *Joy to The World: A Victorian Christmas*. New, York, Workman Publishing Company, Inc., 1990.

Hertz, Louis H. *Messrs. Ives of Bridgeport*. Wethersfield, CT, Mark Haber & Co., 1950.

Hillier, Mary. *Pageant of Toys*. New York, Taplinger Publishing Co., Inc., 1966.

Hockenberry, Dee. **Collectible German Animals Value Guide, 1948-1968**. Cumberland, MD, Hobby House Press, Inc., 1989.

Hornung, Clarence P. *An Old-Fashioned Christmas in Illustration and Decoration*. New York, Dover Publications, Inc., 1975.

Irving, Washington. *Knickerbocker's History of New-York*. New York, George P. Putnam, 1851.

Jones, E. Willis. *The Santa Claus Book*. New York, Walker and Company, 1976.

Kainen, Ruth Cole. *America's Christmas Heritage*. New York, Funk & Wagnalls, 1969.

Kirsch, Francine. *Chromos, A Guide to Paper Collectibles*. La Jolla, CA, A.S. Barnes & Company, Inc., 1981.

Krythe, Mamie R. *All About Christmas*. New York, Harper & Brothers, 1954.

Lavitt, Wendy. *American Folk Dolls*. New York, Alfred A. Knopf, 1982.

McClinton, Katharine Morrison. *Antiques of American Childhood*. New York, Bramhall House, 1970.

Miall, A. and M. *The Victorian Christmas Book*. New York, Pantheon Books, 1978.

Miall, A. and M. *The Victorian Nursery Book*. New York, Pantheon Books, 1980.

Malone, Mary. *Milton Hershey, Chocolate King*. Champaign, IL, Garrard Publishing Company, 1971.

Munch, Peter Andreas. *Norse Mythology*. New York, The American-Scandinavian Foundation, 1963.

Moore, Clement C. *The Night Before Christmas*, [Facsimile of original 1848 edition]. New York, Dover Publications, Inc., 1971.

Nast, Thomas. *Thomas Nast's Christmas Drawings*. New York, Dover Publications, Inc., 1978.

Pistorius, Christel and Rolf. **The Steiff Book**. Cumberland, MD, Hobby House Press, Inc., 1990.

Ray, John B. *Christmas Holidays Around The World.* New York, Comet Press Books, 1959.

Sansom, William. *A Book of Christmas.* New York, McGraw-Hill Book Company, 1968.

Sibley, Brian. *The Land of Narnia.* New York, Harper & Row, Publishers, 1989.

Sieverling, Helen. **3rd Teddy Bear and friends Price Guide**. Cumberland, MD, Hobby House Press, Inc., 1988.

Staff, Frank. *The Picture Postcard and Its Origins.* New York, Frederick A. Praeger, Inc., 1966.

Stevens, Patricia Bunning. *Merry Christmas: A History of The Holiday.* New York, Macmillan Publishing Co., Inc., 1979.

Tennant, Eugenia L. *American Christmases, From The Puritans to The Victorians.* Hicksville, New York, Exposition Press, 1975.

Uttley, Alison. *The Country Child.* London, Faber & Faber, 1931.

Uttley, Alison. *Country Things.* 1946.

Waugh, Carol-Lynn Rössel. **Petite Portraits**. Cumberland, MD, Hobby House Press,Inc., 1982.

Weiser, Francis X. *The Christmas Book.* New York, Harcourt, Brace & Company, 1952.

Whitton, Blair. *American Clockwork Toys, 1862-1900.* Exton, PA, Schiffer Publishing Ltd., 1981.

Whitton, Blair. *Bliss Toys and Dollhouses.* New York, Dover Publications, Inc. and The Margaret Woodbury Strong Museum, 1979.

Whitton, Blair. **Paper Toys of The World**. Cumberland, MD, Hobby House Press, Inc., 1986.

Index